The Way of Mercy

The Way of Mercy

Edited by

CHRISTINE M. BOCHEN

ORBIS BOOKS
Maryknoll, New York 10545

Founded in 1970, Orbis Books endeavors to publish works that enlighten the mind, nourish the spirit, and challenge the conscience. The publishing arm of the Maryknoll Fathers and Brothers, Orbis seeks to explore the global dimensions of the Christian faith and mission, to invite dialogue with diverse cultures and religious traditions, and to serve the cause of reconciliation and peace. The books published reflect the views of their authors and do not represent the official position of the Maryknoll Society. To learn more about Maryknoll and Orbis Books, please visit our website at www.maryknollsociety.org.

Published by Orbis Books, Box 302, Maryknoll, NY 10545-0302.

Manufactured in the United States of America.
Typesetting and book design by Joan Weber Laflamme.

Library of Congress Cataloging-in-Publication Data

Names: Bochen, Christine M., editor. | Catholic Church. Pope (2013– : Francis). Misericordiae Vultus. English.
Title: The way of mercy / Christine M. Bochen, editor.
Description: Maryknoll : Orbis Books, 2016.
Identifiers: LCCN 2015038169 | ISBN 9781626981867 (pbk.)
Subjects: LCSH: Mercy. | Catholic Church—Doctrines.
Classification: LCC BV4647.M4 W39 2016 | DDC 241/.4—dc23
LC record available at http://lccn.loc.gov/2015038169

The Mercy of God

JESSICA POWERS

I am copying down in a book from my
heart's archives
the day that I ceased to fear God with a
shadowy fear.
Would you name it the day that I
measured my column of virtue
and sighted through the windows of
merit a crown that was near?
Ah, no, it was rather the day I began to
see truly
that I came forth from nothing and ever
toward nothingness tend,
that the works of my hands are a
foolishness wrought in the presence
of the worthiest king in a kingdom that
never shall end.
I rose up from the acres of self that I
tended with passion and defended
with flurries of pride;
I walked out of myself and went into the
woods of God's mercy,

From Jessica Powers, *The Selected Poetry of Jessica Powers,* ed. Regina Siegfried, ASC, and Robert R. Morneau (Washington, DC: ICS Publications, 1999), 1.

and here I abide.
There is greenness and calmness and coolness, a soft leafy covering
from the judgment of sun overhead,
and the hush of His peace, and the moss of His mercy to tread.
I have naught but my will seeking God; even love burning in me
is a fragment of infinite loving and never my own.
and I fear God no more; I go forward to wander forever
in a wilderness made of His infinite mercy alone.

Contents

IV
The Works of Mercy

V
Living Mercy

VI
Praying Mercy

Introduction

"Mercy, always, in everything, mercy"

When Thomas Merton penned the words—"mercy, always, in everything, mercy"—in his journal in 1960 he could not have imagined how perfectly they would express the spirit and witness of Pope Francis. Merton's words, formed in prayer, are embodied in the person of Pope Francis for whom, as so many have noted, mercy is the very hallmark of his pontificate and the mark of being a Christian. Thus it is not surprising that Pope Francis should proclaim a Jubilee of Mercy to begin on December 8, 2015—the Solemnity of the Immaculate Conception and the 50th anniversary of the closing of the Second Vatican Council. This choice of opening date underscores Pope Francis' embrace of Pope John XXIII's call for the "medicine of mercy" in the Church and the world. The documents of the Council, most especially the opening words of the *Pastoral Constitution on the Church in the Modern World*, convey an empathy with all of humankind: "The joys and the hopes, the griefs and the anxieties of the men of this age, especially those who are poor or in any way afflicted, these too are the joys and hopes, the griefs and anxieties of the followers of Christ."

These words signaled a new self-understanding on the part of a Church recognizing its responsibility to reach out to all the world with care and compassion. Pope Paul VI echoed the call of Pope John XXIII and the spirit of the Council when in his closing address he noted that the story of the Good Samaritan had been "the model of the spirituality" of the Council.

Pope John Paul II devoted his second encyclical, *Dives in Misericordiae* to the subject of mercy, calling for what Pope

Francis describes as "a more urgent proclamation and witness to mercy in the contemporary world." Pope Benedict declared mercy as "in reality the core of the Gospel message; it is the name of God Himself, the face with which He reveals Himself in the Old Testament and fully in Jesus Christ, the Incarnation of creative and redemptive love." However, it is Pope Francis who from the time he was elected pope has become a living icon of mercy—in words, in gestures, in his very being.

This collection of essays was inspired by and begins with Pope Francis' proclamation of a Jubilee of Mercy. *Misericordiae Vultus—The Face of Mercy*—the papal bull with which Pope Francis announced the Jubilee of Mercy, offers readers a beautiful and profound reflection on mercy—on the God who is Mercy and on Jesus Christ who is "the face of the Father's mercy" and calls each of us to be merciful. We "are called to show mercy," Pope Francis writes, "because mercy has first been shown to us." Such mercy must be "the foundation of the Church's life." The Church, Pope Francis writes, "is commissioned to announce the mercy of God, the beating heart of the Gospel, which in its own way must penetrate the heart and mind of every person." His motto for the Holy Year is simply this: "Merciful like the Father."

The motto is an invitation to open "our hearts to those living on the outermost fringes of society: fringes which modern society itself creates." This demands that we "open our eyes and see the misery of the world, the wounds of our brothers and sisters who are denied their dignity" and "recognize that we are compelled to heed their cry for help." Pope Francis expresses his hope for the Jubilee of Mercy in this way: "May their cry become our own, and together may we break down the barriers of indifference that too often reign supreme and mask our hypocrisy and egoism."

Although the yearlong celebration of the Jubilee of Mercy will come to an end, Pope Francis' insistence on the kerygma of mercy will not—as illustrated by the message in "The

Embrace of God's Mercy"—a homily, one of many, in which Pope Francis touches on the theme of mercy.

Part I of the book concludes with an excerpt from *Pope Francis' Revolution of Tenderness and Love* by Walter Kasper. Readers may recall that Pope Francis read and praised Cardinal Kasper's earlier book, *Mercy: The Essence of the Gospel and the Key to Christian Life.* Cardinal Kasper views mercy as "the key word" of the Pope's pontificate. Noting the centrality of the theme of mercy in the Bible and yet its neglect by Scholastic theology, Kasper points out that Thomas Aquinas saw mercy as "the aspect of God's essence that is turned outward." Justice and mercy are not antithetical; rather, mercy is "God's own justice." Saints such as Catherine of Siena and Thérèse of Lisieux have helped form a tradition of mercy in the Church, as have Pope Francis' immediate predecessors. Nevertheless, Kasper suggests that the "highlighting of mercy" is "a foundational hermeneutical principle" signaling "a paradigm shift" to a method that looks first at "the concrete human situation." As Pope Francis has shown us, "*misericordia* means having a heart for the poor, the poor in the widest and most comprehensive sense. Mercy is about praxis—for the individual and for the church that "is and is supposed to be the sacrament—that is, the sign and instrument of God's mercy."

Part II focuses attention on Jesus and his ethic of mercy. Brazilian theologian Leonardo Boff views mercy and its practice as central to Jesus' proclamation of the reign of God. Jesus embodies the "merciful attitude" of the *Abba-God*—"the Father of infinite mercy." The ethic of Jesus is an ethic of "unlimited love and mercy" that sees the integral connection between the love of God and the love of neighbor—"a love for all without barriers and an unlimited mercy." Jim Forest reflects on the beatitude of mercy proclaimed and modeled by Jesus Christ who is "Mercy itself." After reflecting on the theme of mercy in scripture, Forest observes that mercy is "far from a popular virtue"—illustrating his point with references to the work of writers such as Flannery O'Connor, Dostoevsky, Solzhenitsyn, and Camus. Forest draws on the life of Orthodox saint, Silouan of Mount Athos as well as some contemporary stories to illustrate the transformative power of mercy. "Mercy is a hard virtue," Forest concludes, "even if it sounds like a soft quality. We want mercy for ourselves but resist extending it to others . . . what Christ calls us to become is people living the mercy of God."

Essays by liberation theologian Jon Sobrino and Trappist monk and writer Thomas Merton invite us to reflect on what it means to be a Church of mercy. First published in 1990, in the case of Sobrino, and in 1965, in the case of Merton, the two essays anticipate Pope Francis' vision of Church—something that is also true of other selections in this volume. Sobrino poses a fundamental question: "What is a church that resembles Jesus?" and responds this way: "To resemble Jesus is to reproduce the structure of his life" and to live out the structuring principle of Jesus' life—mercy. Jesus embodies and historicizes the "primordial mercy of God." Mercy, Sobrino insists, is more than the practice of works of mercy. Mercy is "a basic attitude toward the suffering of another, whereby one reacts to eradicate that suffering for the sole reason that it exists, and in the conviction that, in this reaction to the ought-not-be of another's suffering, one's own being, without any possibility of subterfuge, hangs in the balance." This principle of mercy "stands at the origin of all" that Jesus practices. It follows then that it is "this principle of mercy that ought to be operative in Jesus' church" and it is the principle of mercy that ought to govern the church. For Sobrino, the very credibility of the church rests on its being a church of mercy.

Thomas Merton wrote "The Climate of Mercy" for a volume of essays honoring Albert Schweitzer. Mercy, Merton writes, is "the epiphany of hidden truth and of God's redeeming Love for man." God is revealed in Jesus Christ, particularly in the Cross. "To receive mercy and to give it is, then, to participate . . . in the work of the new creation and of redemption." For Merton, the climate of the Christian scriptures is a climate of "the new creation"—a climate "at once of mercy and of life, of forgiveness and creativity." This, he asserts, is the climate that the Church must keep alive. Merton contrasts the climate of mercy with the climate of totalism—a climate of "death and condemnation" in which "men, tribes, nations, sects, parties set themselves up in forms of existence which are mutual accusations" and in which God becomes "a tribal totem." The climate of mercy grows out of the recognition that "*all [people] are acceptable before God* . . . all that is required for a [person] to be acceptable before God . . . is for him to be a man and sinner . . . It is not required that he be a certain type of man, belonging to a special race, or class, even religious customs (Galatians 5:6). Least of all is it required that he be exactly like ourselves." In a world in which greed and love of power are rampant and nuclear weapons are stockpiled, mercy is sorely needed. The function of mercy is eschatological: "to prepare the Christian transformation of the world and to usher in the Kingdom of God." The challenge for the Church is to nurture the climate of mercy in itself and in the world. As might be expected, given Merton's prophetic witness to peace and justice, he writes: "Christian mercy must discover, in faith, in the Spirit, a power strong enough to initiate a transformation of the world into a realm of understanding, unity, and relative peace, where men, nations, and societies are willing to make the enormous sacrifices required if they are to communicate intelligibly with one another, understand one another, cooperate with one another in feeding the hungry millions and in building a world of peace."

Rooted in Scripture and affirmed in early Christian practice and the ongoing development of the Christian tradition, the corporal and spiritual works of mercy express the way of mercy in the form of memorable and proscriptive lists of seven. The corporal works of mercy are: to feed the hungry, to give drink to the thirsty, to clothe the naked, to visit the imprisoned, to shelter the homeless, to visit the sick, and to bury the dead. The spiritual works are: to admonish the sinner, to instruct the ignorant, to counsel the doubtful, to comfort the sorrowful, to bear wrongs patiently, to forgive all injuries, to pray for the living and the dead. In part IV, selections by James F. Keenan, Dorothy Day, and Sidney Callahan invite us to reflect on the works of mercy. Defining mercy as "the willingness to enter into the chaos of the another," Christian ethicist James Keenan observes that "mercy best conveys the actions of God who creates by bringing order out of chaos and who redeems by lifting us out of the chaos of sin" in Christ whose "own entrance into the chaos of death occasions our hope in the risen life." Keenan explains how the early church, monasteries, lay associations and guilds, and religious orders promoted the practice of the corporal works and how the spiritual works developed during the Patristic period. He highlights the contributions of St. Augustine to the understanding and practice of the spiritual works.

In the twentieth century, the Catholic Worker Movement, founded by Peter Maurin and Dorothy Day, came to embody the vision and practice of the corporal and spiritual works of mercy. Dorothy Day's essay, "The Scandal of the Works of Mercy," first published in *The Commonweal* in the November 4, 1949 issue, underscores the centrality of the practice of the works of mercy to being a Christian. "The Works of Mercy are a wonderful stimulus to our growth in faith as well as love," she writes. But she also reminds readers that the practice of the works of mercy is not without cost and trial: "our hearts are often crushed." Nor can that practice be reduced to a single work of mercy: "they all go together." For Dorothy Day, mercy is the measure: "It is by the Works of Mercy that we shall be judged."

Drawing on her work in psychology, ethics, and religion, Sidney Callahan invites us to reflect on what the practice of spiritual works of mercy might look like in our times. In the excerpt included here, she suggests that we practice the spiritual works as persons who ourselves are in need of healing, that our practice may take different forms at different points in our lives, and above all, that we depend on one another in order "to survive and flourish." As ways to express charity, the corporal and spiritual works of mercy challenge us to grow and expand "in undreamed-of directions." Callahan reminds us that acts of mercy do not come "with ready-made patterns to follow"; rather, we discover what mercy—a form of "love in action"—requires of us in particular times, places, and relationships.

The selections in Part V illustrate Sidney Callahan's sense of mercy as lived in the particulars of our life stories. The reflection by Joan Chittister begins with a story of a mother who, thirteen years after her son was murdered, is able to reach out to the man who killed her son. This story becomes the springboard for reflecting on mercy as what God does and what we must also strive to do. Mercy is "what God does for us not because we deserve it but because God loves us." Similarly, we are called to show mercy to others. Mercy reveals both God's divinity and our humanity. In mercy, we become aware of our own humanity, recognizing our weakness and being able to show kindness "to those who are struggling with theirs." It is the practice of mercy that makes us like God or, as mystic Mechtild of Magdeburg, writes: "In so far as we love compassion and practice it steadfastly, to that extent, do we resemble the heavenly Creator who practices these things ceaselessly in us." Sharing insights of St. John Chrysostom, Thomas Aquinas, George Eliot, Sufi mystic Mishkat al-Masabaih, and St. Catherine of Sienna and others, Chittister invites us to reflect on mercy that we might live it ever more fully.

"When God's love touches us in our neediness, the sorrow and suffering inherent in the human condition, we name it mercy," writes Elaine Prevallet. She recalls that the English word mercy is used to translate several Hebrew words including *rahamin,* derived from the word for uterus (*rehem*). Mercy then is "most like womb love"—the love of a mother for the child she carried in her womb. Prevallet turns to Julian of Norwich for whom "mercy was at the very heart of God." Julian, Prevallet explains, uses "spatial, womb-like images" when she describes God's relationship with us. Julian speaks of our being "enclosed" in the Trinity, how God "wraps and enfolds us for love, embraces and shelter us, surrounds us for his love," how Jesus is "our true Mother," how God "shows us our sins by the sweet light of mercy and grace." For Prevallet, as for Julian, God's love is a "mercying love" in which we are called to live. Living in the space of God's "mercying love," we are called to enter into "the suffering, the brokenness, the wounds of humanity that we share in the life of God." In the midst of the violence, injustice and suffering in "an apparently flawed creation," we are called to see "life embraced by a God whose name is Mercy, a God always ready to turn our failings and sins into a capacity for deepened compassion."

The selections in Part VI—reflections by Joyce Rupp and a poem by R. S. Thomas—are explicit invitations to pray for mercy as does Pope Francis in his Prayer for the Jubilee Year of Mercy. However, the call to pray for "mercy, always, in everything mercy," as Merton did, is threaded throughout these selections—and, most especially, in the writings of Pope Francis and in the witness of his life.

I

POPE FRANCIS' CALL TO MERCY

Misericordiae Vultus
The Face of Mercy

Pope Francis

*"May the balm of mercy reach everyone,
both believers and those far away,
as a sign that the Kingdom of God is already present
in our midst!"*

1. Jesus Christ is the face of the Father's mercy. These words might well sum up the mystery of the Christian faith. Mercy has become living and visible in Jesus of Nazareth, reaching its culmination in him. The Father, "rich in mercy" (Eph 2:4), after having revealed his name to Moses as "a God merciful and gracious, slow to anger, and abounding in steadfast love and faithfulness" (Ex 34:6), has never ceased to show, in various ways throughout history, his divine nature. In the "fullness of time" (Gal 4:4), when everything had been arranged according to his plan of salvation, he sent his only Son into the world, born of the Virgin Mary, to reveal his love for us in a definitive way. Whoever sees Jesus sees the Father (cf. Jn 14:9). Jesus of Nazareth, by his words, his actions, and his entire person[1] reveals the mercy of God.

2. We need constantly to contemplate the mystery of mercy. It is a wellspring of joy, serenity, and peace. Our salvation

---

From Pope Francis, "*Misericordiae Vultus*—Bull of Indiction of the Extraordinary Jubilee of Mercy." Vatican: The Holy See. Rome, 11 April 2015.

depends on it. Mercy: the word reveals the very mystery of the Most Holy Trinity. Mercy: the ultimate and supreme act by which God comes to meet us. Mercy: the fundamental law that dwells in the heart of every person who looks sincerely into the eyes of his brothers and sisters on the path of life. Mercy: the bridge that connects God and man, opening our hearts to the hope of being loved forever despite our sinfulness.

3. At times we are called to gaze even more attentively on mercy so that we may become a more effective sign of the Father's action in our lives. For this reason I have proclaimed an *Extraordinary Jubilee of Mercy* as a special time for the Church, a time when the witness of believers might grow stronger and more effective.

The Holy Year will open on 8 December 2015, the Solemnity of the Immaculate Conception. This liturgical feast day recalls God's action from the very beginning of the history of mankind. After the sin of Adam and Eve, God did not wish to leave humanity alone in the throes of evil. And so he turned his gaze to Mary, holy and immaculate in love (cf. Eph 1:4), choosing her to be the Mother of man's Redeemer. When faced with the gravity of sin, God responds with the fullness of mercy. Mercy will always be greater than any sin, and no one can place limits on the love of God who is ever ready to forgive. I will have the joy of opening the Holy Door on the Solemnity of the Immaculate Conception. On that day, the Holy Door will become a *Door of Mercy* through which anyone who enters will experience the love of God who consoles, pardons, and instills hope.

On the following Sunday, the Third Sunday of Advent, the Holy Door of the Cathedral of Rome—that is, the Basilica of Saint John Lateran—will be opened. In the following weeks, the Holy Doors of the other Papal Basilicas will be opened. On the same Sunday, I will announce that in every local church, at the cathedral—the mother church of the faithful in any particular area—or, alternatively, at the co-cathedral or another church of special significance, a Door of Mercy will be opened for the duration of the Holy Year. At the discretion of the local ordinary, a similar door may be opened at any shrine frequented by large groups of pilgrims, since visits to these holy sites are so often grace-filled moments, as people discover a path to conversion. Every Particular Church, therefore, will be directly involved in living out this Holy Year as an extraordinary moment of grace and spiritual renewal. Thus the Jubilee will be celebrated both in Rome and in the Particular Churches as a visible sign of the Church's universal communion.

4. I have chosen the date of 8 December because of its rich meaning in the recent history of the Church. In fact, I will open the Holy Door on the fiftieth anniversary of the closing of the Second Vatican Ecumenical Council. The Church feels a great need to keep this event alive. With the Council, the Church entered a new phase of her history. The Council Fathers strongly perceived, as a true breath of the Holy Spirit, a need to talk about God to men and women of their time in a more accessible way. The walls which for too long had made the Church a kind of fortress were torn down and the time had come to proclaim the Gospel in a new way. It was a new phase of the same evangelization that had existed from the beginning. It was a fresh undertaking for all Christians to bear witness to their faith with greater enthusiasm and conviction. The Church sensed a responsibility to be a living sign of the Father's love in the world.

We recall the poignant words of Saint John XXIII when, opening the Council, he indicated the path to follow: "Now the Bride of Christ wishes to use the medicine of mercy rather than taking up arms of severity. . . . The Catholic Church, as she holds high the torch of Catholic truth at this Ecumenical Council, wants to show herself a loving mother to all; patient, kind, moved by compassion and goodness toward her separated children."[2] Blessed Paul VI spoke in a similar vein at the closing of the Council: "We prefer to point out how charity has been the principal religious feature of this Council . . . the old story of the Good Samaritan has been the model of the spirituality of the Council . . . a wave of affection and admiration flowed from the Council over the modern world of humanity. Errors were condemned, indeed, because charity demanded this no less than did truth, but for individuals themselves there was only admonition, respect and love. Instead of depressing diagnoses, encouraging remedies; instead of direful predictions, messages of trust issued from the Council to the present-day world. The modern world's values were not only respected but honoured, its efforts approved, its aspirations purified and blessed. . . . Another point we must stress is this: all this rich teaching is channelled in one direction, the service of mankind, of every condition, in every weakness and need."[3]

With these sentiments of gratitude for everything the Church has received, and with a sense of responsibility for the task that lies ahead, we shall cross the threshold of the Holy Door fully confident that the strength of the Risen Lord, who constantly supports us on our pilgrim way, will sustain us. May the Holy Spirit, who guides the steps of believers in cooperating with the work of salvation wrought by Christ, lead the way and support the People of God so that they may contemplate the face of mercy.[4]

5. The Jubilee year will close with the liturgical Solemnity of Christ the King on 20 November 2016. On that day, as we seal the Holy Door, we shall be filled, above all, with a sense of gratitude and thanksgiving to the Most Holy Trinity for having granted us an extraordinary time of grace. We will entrust the life of the Church, all humanity, and the entire cosmos to the Lordship of Christ, asking him to pour out his mercy upon us like the morning dew, so that everyone may work together to build a brighter future. How much I desire that the year to come will be steeped in mercy, so that we can go out to every man and woman, bringing the goodness and tenderness of God! May the balm of mercy reach everyone, both believers and those far

away, as a sign that the Kingdom of God is already present in our midst!

6. "It is proper to God to exercise mercy, and he manifests his omnipotence particularly in this way."[5] Saint Thomas Aquinas' words show that God's mercy, rather than a sign of weakness, is the mark of his omnipotence. For this reason the liturgy, in one of its most ancient collects, has us pray: "O God, who reveal your power above all in your mercy and forgiveness . . . "[6] Throughout the history of humanity, God will always be the One who is present, close, provident, holy, and merciful.

"Patient and merciful." These words often go together in the Old Testament to describe God's nature. His being merciful is concretely demonstrated in his many actions throughout the history of salvation where his goodness prevails over punishment and destruction. In a special way the Psalms bring to the fore the grandeur of his merciful action: "He forgives all your iniquity, he heals all your diseases, he redeems your life from the pit, he crowns you with steadfast love and mercy" (Ps 103:3–4). Another psalm, in an even more explicit way, attests to the concrete signs of his mercy: "He executes justice for the oppressed; he gives food to the hungry. The Lord sets the prisoners free; the Lord opens the eyes of the blind. The Lord lifts up those who are bowed down; the Lord loves the righteous. The Lord watches over the sojourners, he upholds the widow and the fatherless; but the way of the wicked he brings to ruin" (Ps 146:7–9). Here are some other expressions of the Psalmist: "He heals the brokenhearted, and binds up their wounds. . . . The Lord lifts up the downtrodden, he casts the wicked to the ground" (Ps 147:3, 6). In short, the mercy of God is not an abstract idea, but a concrete reality with which he reveals his love as of that of a father or a mother, moved to the very depths out of love for their child. It is hardly an exaggeration to say that this is a "visceral" love. It gushes forth from the depths naturally, full of tenderness and compassion, indulgence and mercy.

7. "For his mercy endures forever." This is the refrain that repeats after each verse in Psalm 136 as it narrates the history of God's revelation. By virtue of mercy, all the events of the Old Testament are replete with profound salvific import. Mercy renders God's history with Israel a history of salvation. To repeat continually "for his mercy endures forever," as the psalm does, seems to break through the dimensions of space and time, inserting everything into the eternal mystery of love. It is as if to say that not only in history, but for all eternity man will always be under the merciful gaze of the Father. It is no accident that the people of Israel wanted to include this psalm—the "Great *Hallel*," as it is called—in its most important liturgical feast days.

Before his Passion, Jesus prayed with this psalm of mercy. Matthew attests to this in his Gospel when he says that, "when they had sung a hymn" (26:30), Jesus and his disciples went out to the Mount of Olives. While he was instituting the Eucharist as an everlasting memorial of himself and his paschal sacrifice, he symbolically placed this supreme act of revelation in the light of his mercy. Within the very same context of mercy, Jesus entered upon his passion and death, conscious of the great mystery of love that he would consummate on the Cross. Knowing that Jesus himself prayed this psalm makes it even more important for us as Christians, challenging us to take up the refrain in our daily lives by praying these words of praise: "for his mercy endures forever."

8. With our eyes fixed on Jesus and his merciful gaze, we experience the love of the Most Holy Trinity. The mission Jesus received from the Father was that of revealing the mystery of divine love in its fullness. "God is love" (1 Jn 4:8,16), John affirms for the first and only time in all of Holy Scripture. This love has now been made visible and tangible in Jesus' entire life. His person is nothing but love, a love given gratuitously. The relationships he forms with the people who approach him manifest something entirely

unique and unrepeatable. The signs he works, especially in favour of sinners, the poor, the marginalized, the sick, and the suffering, are all meant to teach mercy. Everything in him speaks of mercy. Nothing in him is devoid of compassion.

Jesus, seeing the crowds of people who followed him, realized that they were tired and exhausted, lost and without a guide, and he felt deep compassion for them (cf. Mt 9:36). On the basis of this compassionate love he healed the sick who were presented to him (cf. Mt 14:14), and with just a few loaves of bread and fish he satisfied the enormous crowd (cf. Mt 15:37). What moved Jesus in all of these situations was nothing other than mercy, with which he read the hearts of those he encountered and responded to their deepest need. When he came upon the widow of Nain taking her son out for burial, he felt great compassion for the immense suffering of this grieving mother, and he gave back her son by raising him from the dead (cf. Lk 7:15). After freeing the demoniac in the country of the Gerasenes, Jesus entrusted him with this mission: "Go home to your friends, and tell them how much the Lord has done for you, and how he has had mercy on you" (Mk 5:19). The calling of Matthew is also presented within the context of mercy. Passing by the tax collector's booth, Jesus looked intently at Matthew. It was a look full of mercy that forgave the sins of that man, a sinner and a tax collector, whom Jesus chose—against the hesitation of the disciples—to become one of the Twelve. Saint Bede the Venerable, commenting on this Gospel passage, wrote that Jesus looked upon Matthew with merciful love and chose him: *miserando atque eligendo*.[7] This expression impressed me so much that I chose it for my episcopal motto.

9. In the parables devoted to mercy, Jesus reveals the nature of God as that of a Father who never gives up until he has forgiven the wrong and overcome rejection with compassion and mercy. We know these parables well, three in particular:

the lost sheep, the lost coin, and the father with two sons (cf. Lk 15:1–32). In these parables, God is always presented as full of joy, especially when he pardons. In them we find the core of the Gospel and of our faith, because mercy is presented as a force that overcomes everything, filling the heart with love and bringing consolation through pardon.

From another parable, we cull an important teaching for our Christian lives. In reply to Peter's question about how many times it is necessary to forgive, Jesus says: "I do not say seven times, but seventy times seven times" (Mt 18:22). He then goes on to tell the parable of the "ruthless servant," who, called by his master to return a huge amount, begs him on his knees for mercy. His master cancels his debt. But he then meets a fellow servant who owes him a few cents and who in turn begs on his knees for mercy, but the first servant refuses his request and throws him into jail. When the master hears of the matter, he becomes infuriated and, summoning the first servant back to him, says, "Should not you have had mercy on your fellow servant, as I had mercy on you?" (Mt 18:33). Jesus concludes, "So also my heavenly Father will do to every one of you, if you do not forgive your brother from your heart" (Mt 18:35).

This parable contains a profound teaching for all of us. Jesus affirms that mercy is not only an action of the Father, it becomes a criterion for ascertaining who his true children are. In short, we are called to show mercy because mercy has first been shown to us. Pardoning offences becomes the clearest expression of merciful love, and for us Christians it is an imperative from which we cannot excuse ourselves. At times how hard it seems to forgive! And yet pardon is the instrument placed into our fragile hands to attain serenity of heart. To let go of anger, wrath, violence, and revenge are necessary conditions to living joyfully. Let us therefore heed the Apostle's exhortation: "Do not let the sun go down on your anger" (Eph 4:26). Above all, let us listen to the words of Jesus who made mercy an ideal of life and a criterion for the credibility of our faith: "Blessed are the merciful, for they shall obtain mercy" (Mt 5:7): the beatitude to which we should particularly aspire in this Holy Year.

As we can see in Sacred Scripture, mercy is a key word that indicates God's action towards us. He does not limit himself merely to affirming his love, but makes it visible and tangible. Love, after all, can never be just an abstraction. By its very nature, it indicates something concrete: intentions, attitudes, and behaviours that are shown in daily living. The mercy of God is his loving concern for each one of us. He feels responsible; that is, he desires our wellbeing and he wants to see us happy, full of joy, and peaceful. This is the path which the merciful love of Christians must also travel. As the Father loves, so do his children. Just as he is merciful, so we are called to be merciful to each other.

10. Mercy is the very foundation of the Church's life. All of her pastoral activity should be caught up in the tenderness she makes present to believers; nothing in her preaching and in her witness to the world can be lacking in mercy. The Church's very credibility is seen in how she shows merciful and compassionate love. The Church "has an endless desire to show mercy."[8] Perhaps we have long since forgotten how to show and live the way of mercy. The temptation, on the one hand, to focus exclusively on justice made us forget that this is only the first, albeit necessary and indispensable step. But the Church needs to go beyond and strive for a higher and more important goal. On the other hand, sad to say, we must admit that the practice of mercy is waning in the wider culture. In some cases the word seems to have dropped out of use. However, without a witness to mercy, life becomes fruitless and sterile, as if sequestered in a barren desert. The time has come for the Church to take up the joyful call to mercy once more. It is time to return to the basics and to bear the weaknesses and struggles of our brothers and sisters. Mercy is the force that reawakens us to new life and instils in us the courage to look to the future with hope.

11. Let us not forget the great teaching offered by Saint John Paul II in his second Encyclical, *Dives in Misericordia*, which at the time came unexpectedly, its theme catching many by surprise. There are two passages in particular to which I would like to draw attention. First, Saint John Paul II highlighted the fact that we had forgotten the theme of mercy in today's cultural milieu: "The present-day mentality, more perhaps than that of people in the past, seems opposed to a God of mercy, and in fact tends to exclude from life and to remove from the human heart the very idea of mercy. The word and the concept of 'mercy' seem to cause uneasiness in man, who, thanks to the enormous development of science and technology, never before known in history, has become the master of the earth and has subdued and dominated it (cf. Gen 1:28). This dominion over the earth, sometimes understood in a one-sided and superficial way, seems to have no room for mercy. . . . And this is why, in the situation of the Church and the world today, many individuals and groups guided by a lively sense of faith are turning, I would say almost spontaneously, to the mercy of God."[9]

Furthermore, Saint John Paul II pushed for a more urgent proclamation and witness to mercy in the contemporary world: "It is dictated by love for man, for all that is human and which, according to the intuitions of many of our contemporaries, is threatened by an immense danger. The mystery of Christ . . . obliges me to proclaim mercy as God's merciful love, revealed in that same mystery of Christ. It likewise obliges me to have recourse to that mercy and to beg for it at this difficult, critical phase of the history of the Church and of the world."[10] This teaching is more pertinent than ever and deserves to be taken up once again in this Holy Year. Let us listen to his words once more: "The Church lives an authentic life when she professes and proclaims mercy—the most stupendous attribute of the Creator and of the Redeemer—and when she brings people close to the sources of the Saviour's mercy, of which she is the trustee and dispenser."[11]

12. The Church is commissioned to announce the mercy of God, the beating heart of the Gospel, which in its own way must penetrate the heart and mind of every person. The Spouse of Christ must pattern her behaviour after the Son of God who went out to everyone without exception. In the present day, as the Church is charged with the task of the new evangelization, the theme of mercy needs to be proposed again and again with new enthusiasm and renewed pastoral action. It is absolutely essential for the Church and for the credibility of her message that she herself live and testify to mercy. Her language and her gestures must transmit mercy, so as to touch the hearts of all people and inspire them once more to find the road that leads to the Father.

The Church's first truth is the love of Christ. The Church makes herself a servant of this love and mediates it to all people: a love that forgives and expresses itself in the gift of oneself. Consequently, wherever the Church is present, the mercy of the Father must be evident. In our parishes, communities, associations and movements, in a word, wherever there are Christians, everyone should find an oasis of mercy.

13. We want to live this Jubilee Year in light of the Lord's words: *Merciful like the Father.* The Evangelist reminds us of the teaching of Jesus who says, "Be merciful just as your Father is merciful" (Lk 6:36). It is a programme of life as demanding as it is rich with joy and peace. Jesus's command is directed to anyone willing to listen to his voice (cf. Lk 6:27). In order to be capable of mercy, therefore, we must first of all dispose ourselves to listen to the Word of God. This means rediscovering the value of silence in order to meditate on the Word that comes to us. In this way, it will be possible to contemplate God's mercy and adopt it as our lifestyle.

14. The practice of *pilgrimage* has a special place in the Holy Year, because it represents the journey each of us makes in this life. Life itself is a pilgrimage, and the human

being is a *viator*, a pilgrim travelling along the road, making his way to the desired destination. Similarly, to reach the Holy Door in Rome or in any other place in the world, everyone, each according to his or her ability, will have to make a pilgrimage. This will be a sign that mercy is also a goal to reach and requires dedication and sacrifice. May pilgrimage be an impetus to conversion: by crossing the threshold of the Holy Door, we will find the strength to embrace God's mercy and dedicate ourselves to being merciful with others as the Father has been with us.

The Lord Jesus shows us the steps of the pilgrimage to attain our goal: "Judge not, and you will not be judged; condemn not, and you will not be condemned; forgive, and you will be forgiven; give, and it will be given to you; good measure, pressed down, shaken together, running over, will be put into your lap. For the measure you give will be the measure you get back" (Lk 6:37–38). The Lord asks us above all *not to judge* and *not to condemn*. If anyone wishes to avoid God's judgement, he should not make himself the judge of his brother or sister. Human beings, whenever they judge, look no farther than the surface, whereas the Father looks into the very depths of the soul. How much harm words do when they are motivated by feelings of jealousy and envy! To speak ill of others puts them in a bad light, undermines their reputation and leaves them prey to the whims of gossip. To refrain from judgement and condemnation means, in a positive sense, to know how to accept the good in every person and to spare him any suffering that might be caused by our partial judgment, our presumption to know everything about him. But this is still not sufficient to express mercy. Jesus asks us also to *forgive* and to *give*. To be instruments of mercy because it was we who first received mercy from God. To be generous with others, knowing that God showers his goodness upon us with immense generosity.

Merciful like the Father, therefore, is the "motto" of this Holy Year. In mercy, we find proof of how God loves us. He gives his entire self, always, freely, asking nothing in return. He comes to our aid whenever we call upon him. What a beautiful thing that the Church begins her daily prayer with the words, "O God, come to my assistance. O Lord, make haste to help me" (Ps 70:2)! The assistance we ask for is already the first step of God's mercy toward us. He comes to assist us in our weakness. And his help consists in helping us accept his presence and closeness to us. Day after day, touched by his compassion, we also can become compassionate towards others.

15. In this Holy Year, we look forward to the experience of opening our hearts to those living on the outermost fringes of society: fringes which modern society itself creates. How many uncertain and painful situations there are in the world today! How many are the wounds borne by the flesh of those who have no voice because their cry is muffled and drowned out by the indifference of the rich! During this Jubilee, the Church will be called even more to heal these wounds, to assuage them with the oil of consolation, to bind them with mercy and cure them with solidarity and vigilant care. Let us not fall into humiliating indifference or a monotonous routine that prevents us from discovering what is new! Let us ward off destructive cynicism! Let us open our eyes and see the misery of the world, the wounds of our brothers and sisters who are denied their dignity, and let us recognize that we are compelled to heed their cry for help! May we reach out to them and support them so they can feel the warmth of our presence, our friendship, and our fraternity! May their cry become our own, and together may we break down the barriers of indifference that too often reign supreme and mask our hypocrisy and egoism!

It is my burning desire that, during this Jubilee, the Christian people may reflect on the *corporal and spiritual works of mercy*. It will be a way to reawaken our conscience, too often grown dull in the face of poverty. And let us enter more deeply into the heart of the Gospel where the poor have a special experience of God's mercy. Jesus introduces us to these works of mercy in his preaching so that we can know whether or not we are living as his disciples. Let us rediscover these *corporal works of mercy*: to feed the hungry, give drink to the thirsty, clothe the naked, welcome the stranger, heal the sick, visit the imprisoned, and bury the dead. And let us not forget the *spiritual works of mercy:* to counsel the doubtful, instruct the ignorant, admonish sinners, comfort the afflicted, forgive offences, bear patiently those who do us ill, and pray for the living and the dead.

We cannot escape the Lord's words to us, and they will serve as the criteria upon which we will be judged: whether we have fed the hungry and given drink to the thirsty, welcomed the stranger and clothed the naked, or spent time with the sick and those in prison (cf. Mt 25:31–45). Moreover, we will be asked if we have helped others to escape the doubt that causes them to fall into despair and which is often a source of loneliness; if we have helped to overcome the ignorance in which millions of people live, especially children deprived of the necessary means to free them from the bonds of poverty; if we have been close to the lonely and afflicted; if we have forgiven those who have offended us and have rejected all forms of anger and hate that lead to violence; if we have had the kind of patience God shows, who is so patient with us; and if we have commended our brothers and sisters to the Lord in prayer. In each of these "little ones," Christ himself is present. His flesh becomes visible in the flesh of the tortured, the crushed, the scourged, the malnourished, and the exiled . . . to be acknowledged, touched, and cared for by us. Let us not forget the words of Saint John of the Cross: "as we prepare to leave this life, we will be judged on the basis of love."[12]

16. In the Gospel of Luke, we find another important element that will help us live the Jubilee with faith. Luke writes that Jesus, on the Sabbath, went back to Nazareth and, as was his custom, entered the synagogue. They called upon

him to read the Scripture and to comment on it. The passage was from the Book of Isaiah where it is written: "The Spirit of the Lord God is upon me, because the Lord has anointed me to bring good tidings to the afflicted; he has sent me to bind up the brokenhearted, to proclaim liberty to the captives, and freedom to those in captivity; to proclaim the year of the Lord's favour" (Is 61:1–2). A "year of the Lord's favour" or "mercy": this is what the Lord proclaimed and this is what we wish to live now. This Holy Year will bring to the fore the richness of Jesus' mission echoed in the words of the prophet: to bring a word and gesture of consolation to the poor, to proclaim liberty to those bound by new forms of slavery in modern society, to restore sight to those who can see no more because they are caught up in themselves, to restore dignity to all those from whom it has been robbed. The preaching of Jesus is made visible once more in the response of faith which Christians are called to offer by their witness. May the words of the Apostle accompany us: he who does acts of mercy, let him do them with cheerfulness (cf. Rom 12:8).

17. The season of Lent during this Jubilee Year should also be lived more intensely as a privileged moment to celebrate and experience God's mercy. How many pages of Sacred Scripture are appropriate for meditation during the weeks of Lent to help us rediscover the merciful face of the Father! We can repeat the words of the prophet Micah and make them our own: You, O Lord, are a God who takes away iniquity and pardons sin, who does not hold your anger forever, but are pleased to show mercy. You, Lord, will return to us and have pity on your people. You will trample down our sins and toss them into the depths of the sea (cf. 7:18–19).

The pages of the prophet Isaiah can also be meditated upon concretely during this season of prayer, fasting, and works of charity: "Is not this the fast that I choose: to loosen the bonds of wickedness, to undo the thongs of the yoke, to let the oppressed go free, and to break every yoke? Is it not to share your bread with the hungry, and bring the homeless poor into your house; when you see the naked, to cover him, and not to hide yourself from your own flesh? Then shall your light break forth like the dawn, and your healing shall spring up speedily; your righteousness shall go before you, the glory of the Lord shall be your rear guard. Then you shall call, and the Lord will answer; you shall cry, and he will say, here I am. If you take away from the midst of you the yoke, the pointing of the finger, and speaking wickedness, if you pour yourself out for the hungry and satisfy the desire of the afflicted, then shall your light rise in the darkness and your gloom be as the noonday. And the Lord will guide you continually, and satisfy your desire with good things, and make your bones strong; and you shall be like a watered garden, like a spring of water, whose waters fail not" (58:6–11).

The initiative of "*24 Hours for the Lord*," to be celebrated on the Friday and Saturday preceding the Fourth Week of Lent, should be implemented in every diocese. So many people, including young people, are returning to the Sacrament of Reconciliation; through this experience they are rediscovering a path back to the Lord, living a moment of intense prayer and finding meaning in their lives. Let us place the Sacrament of Reconciliation at the centre once more in such a way that it will enable people to touch the grandeur of God's mercy with their own hands. For every penitent, it will be a source of true interior peace.

I will never tire of insisting that confessors be authentic signs of the Father's mercy. We do not become good confessors automatically. We become good confessors when, above all, we allow ourselves to be penitents in search of his mercy. Let us never forget that to be confessors means to participate in the very mission of Jesus to be a concrete sign of the constancy of divine love that pardons and saves. We priests have received the gift of the Holy Spirit for the forgiveness of sins, and we are responsible for this. None of us wields power over this Sacrament; rather, we are faithful servants of God's mercy through it. Every confessor must accept the faithful as the father in the parable of the prodigal son: a father who runs out to meet his son despite the fact that he has squandered away his inheritance. Confessors are called to embrace the repentant son who comes back home and to express the joy of having him back again. Let us never tire of also going out to the other son who stands outside, incapable of rejoicing, in order to explain to him that his judgement is severe and unjust and meaningless in light of the father's boundless mercy. May confessors not ask useless questions, but like the father in the parable, interrupt the speech prepared ahead of time by the prodigal son, so that confessors will learn to accept the plea for help and mercy pouring from the heart of every penitent. In short, confessors are called to be a sign of the primacy of mercy always, everywhere, and in every situation, no matter what.

18. During Lent of this Holy Year, I intend to send out *Missionaries of Mercy*. They will be a sign of the Church's maternal solicitude for the People of God, enabling them to enter the profound richness of this mystery so fundamental to the faith. There will be priests to whom I will grant the authority to pardon even those sins reserved to the Holy See, so that the breadth of their mandate as confessors will be even clearer. They will be, above all, living signs of the Father's readiness to welcome those in search of his pardon. They will be missionaries of mercy because they will be facilitators of a truly human encounter, a source of liberation, rich with responsibility for overcoming obstacles and taking up the new life of Baptism again. They will be led in their mission by the words of the Apostle: "For God has consigned all men to disobedience, that he may have mercy upon all" (Rom 11:32). Everyone, in fact, without exception, is called to embrace the call to mercy. May these Missionaries live this call with the assurance that they can fix their eyes on Jesus, "the merciful and faithful high priest in the service of God" (Heb 2:17).

I ask my brother Bishops to invite and welcome these Missionaries so that they can be, above all, persuasive preachers of mercy. May individual dioceses organize "missions to the people" in such a way that these Missionaries may be heralds of joy and forgiveness. Bishops are asked to celebrate the Sacrament of Reconciliation with their people so that the time of grace made possible by the Jubilee year makes it possible for many of God's sons and daughters to take up once again the journey to the Father's house. May pastors, especially during the liturgical season of Lent, be diligent in calling back the faithful "to the throne of grace, that we may receive mercy and find grace" (Heb 4:16).

19. May the message of mercy reach everyone, and may no one be indifferent to the call to experience mercy. I direct this invitation to conversion even more fervently to those whose behaviour distances them from the grace of God. I particularly have in mind men and women belonging to criminal organizations of any kind. For their own good, I beg them to change their lives. I ask them this in the name of the Son of God who, though rejecting sin, never rejected the sinner. Do not fall into the terrible trap of thinking that life depends on money and that, in comparison with money, anything else is devoid of value or dignity. This is nothing but an illusion! We cannot take money with us into the life beyond. Money does not bring us happiness. Violence inflicted for the sake of amassing riches soaked in blood makes one neither powerful nor immortal. Everyone, sooner or later, will be subject to God's judgment, from which no one can escape.

The same invitation is extended to those who either perpetrate or participate in corruption. This festering wound is a grave sin that cries out to heaven for vengeance, because it threatens the very foundations of personal and social life. Corruption prevents us from looking to the future with hope, because its tyrannical greed shatters the plans of the weak and tramples upon the poorest of the poor. It is an evil that embeds itself into the actions of everyday life and spreads, causing great public scandal. Corruption is a sinful hardening of the heart that replaces God with the illusion that money is a form of power. It is a work of darkness, fed by suspicion and intrigue. *Corruptio optimi pessima*, Saint Gregory the Great said with good reason, affirming that no one can think himself immune from this temptation. If we want to drive it out from personal and social life, we need prudence, vigilance, loyalty, transparency, together with the courage to denounce any wrongdoing. If it is not combated openly, sooner or later everyone will become an accomplice to it, and it will end up destroying our very existence.

This is the opportune moment to change our lives! This is the time to allow our hearts to be touched! When faced with evil deeds, even in the face of serious crimes, it is the time to listen to the cry of innocent people who are deprived of their property, their dignity, their feelings, and even their very lives. To stick to the way of evil will only leave one deluded and sad. True life is something entirely different. God never tires of reaching out to us. He is always ready to listen, as I am too, along with my brother bishops and priests. All one needs to do is to accept the invitation to conversion and submit oneself to justice during this special time of mercy offered by the Church.

20. It would not be out of place at this point to recall the relationship between *justice* and *mercy*. These are not two contradictory realities, but two dimensions of a single reality that unfolds progressively until it culminates in the fullness of love. Justice is a fundamental concept for civil society, which is meant to be governed by the rule of law. Justice is also understood as that which is rightly due to each individual. In the Bible, there are many references to divine justice and to God as "judge." In these passages, justice is understood as the full observance of the Law and the behaviour of every good Israelite in conformity with God's commandments. Such a vision, however, has not infrequently

led to legalism by distorting the original meaning of justice and obscuring its profound value. To overcome this legalistic perspective, we need to recall that in Sacred Scripture, justice is conceived essentially as the faithful abandonment of oneself to God's will.

For his part, Jesus speaks several times of the importance of faith over and above the observance of the law. It is in this sense that we must understand his words when, reclining at table with Matthew and other tax collectors and sinners, he says to the Pharisees raising objections to him, "Go and learn the meaning of 'I desire mercy not sacrifice'. I have come not to call the righteous, but sinners" (Mt 9:13). Faced with a vision of justice as the mere observance of the law that judges people simply by dividing them into two groups—the just and sinners—Jesus is bent on revealing the great gift of mercy that searches out sinners and offers them pardon and salvation. One can see why, on the basis of such a liberating vision of mercy as a source of new life, Jesus was rejected by the Pharisees and the other teachers of the law. In an attempt to remain faithful to the law, they merely placed burdens on the shoulders of others and undermined the Father's mercy. The appeal to a faithful observance of the law must not prevent attention from being given to matters that touch upon the dignity of the person.

The appeal Jesus makes to the text from the book of the prophet Hosea—"I desire love and not sacrifice" (6:6)—is important in this regard. Jesus affirms that, from that time onward, the rule of life for his disciples must place mercy at the centre, as Jesus himself demonstrated by sharing meals with sinners. Mercy, once again, is revealed as a fundamental aspect of Jesus' mission. This is truly challenging to his hearers, who would draw the line at a formal respect for the law. Jesus, on the other hand, goes beyond the law; the company he keeps with those the law considers sinners makes us realize the depth of his mercy.

The Apostle Paul makes a similar journey. Prior to meeting Jesus on the road to Damascus, he dedicated his life to pursuing the justice of the law with zeal (cf. Phil 3:6). His conversion to Christ led him to turn that vision upside down, to the point that he would write to the Galatians: "We have believed in Christ Jesus, in order to be justified by faith in Christ, and not by works of the law, because by works of the law shall no one be justified" (2:16).

Paul's understanding of justice changes radically. He now places faith first, not justice. Salvation comes not through the observance of the law, but through faith in Jesus Christ, who in his death and resurrection brings salvation together with a mercy that justifies. God's justice now becomes the liberating force for those oppressed by slavery to sin and its consequences. God's justice is his mercy (cf. Ps 51:11–16).

21. Mercy is not opposed to justice but rather expresses God's way of reaching out to the sinner, offering him a new chance to look at himself, convert, and believe. The experience of the prophet Hosea can help us see the way in which mercy surpasses justice. The era in which the prophet lived was one of the most dramatic in the history of the Jewish people. The kingdom was tottering on the edge of destruction; the people had not remained faithful to the covenant; they had wandered from God and lost the faith of their forefathers. According to human logic, it seems reasonable for God to think of rejecting an unfaithful people; they had not observed their pact with God and therefore deserved just punishment: in other words, exile. The prophet's words attest to this: "They shall not return to the land of Egypt, and Assyria shall be their king, because they have refused to return to me" (Hos11:5). And yet, after this invocation of justice, the prophet radically changes his speech and reveals the true face of God: "How can I give you up, O Ephraim! How can I hand you over, O Israel! How can I make you like Admah! How can I treat you like Zeboiim! My heart recoils within me, my compassion grows warm and tender. I will not execute

my fierce anger, I will not again destroy Ephraim; for I am God and not man, the Holy One in your midst, and I will not come to destroy" (11:8–9). Saint Augustine, almost as if he were commenting on these words of the prophet, says: "It is easier for God to hold back anger than mercy."[13] And so it is. God's anger lasts but a moment, his mercy forever.

If God limited himself to only justice, he would cease to be God, and would instead be like human beings who ask merely that the law be respected. But mere justice is not enough. Experience shows that an appeal to justice alone will result in its destruction. This is why God goes beyond justice with his mercy and forgiveness. Yet this does not mean that justice should be devalued or rendered superfluous. On the contrary: anyone who makes a mistake must pay the price. However, this is just the beginning of conversion, not its end, because one begins to feel the tenderness and mercy of God. God does not deny justice. He rather envelopes it and surpasses it with an even greater event in which we experience love as the foundation of true justice. We must pay close attention to what Saint Paul says if we want to avoid making the same mistake for which he reproaches the Jews of his time: "For, being ignorant of the righteousness that comes from God, and seeking to establish their own, they did not submit to God's righteousness. For Christ is the end of the law, that everyone who has faith may be justified" (Rom 10:3–4). God's justice is his mercy given to everyone as a grace that flows from the death and resurrection of Jesus Christ. Thus the Cross of Christ is God's judgement on all of us and on the whole world, because through it he offers us the certitude of love and new life.

22. A Jubilee also entails the granting of *indulgences*. This practice will acquire an even more important meaning in the Holy Year of Mercy. God's forgiveness knows no bounds. In the death and resurrection of Jesus Christ, God makes even more evident his love and its power to destroy all human

sin. Reconciliation with God is made possible through the paschal mystery and the mediation of the Church. Thus God is always ready to forgive, and he never tires of forgiving in ways that are continually new and surprising. Nevertheless, all of us know well the experience of sin. We know that we are called to perfection (cf. Mt 5:48), yet we feel the heavy burden of sin. Though we feel the transforming power of grace, we also feel the effects of sin typical of our fallen state. Despite being forgiven, the conflicting consequences of our sins remain. In the Sacrament of Reconciliation, God forgives our sins, which he truly blots out; and yet sin leaves a negative effect on the way we think and act. But the mercy of God is stronger even than this. It becomes indulgence on the part of the Father who, through the Bride of Christ, his Church, reaches the pardoned sinner and frees him from every residue left by the consequences of sin, enabling him to act with charity, to grow in love rather than to fall back into sin.

The Church lives within the communion of the saints. In the Eucharist, this communion, which is a gift from God, becomes a spiritual union binding us to the saints and blessed ones whose number is beyond counting (cf. Rev 7:4). Their holiness comes to the aid of our weakness in a way that enables the Church, with her maternal prayers and her way of life, to fortify the weakness of some with the strength of others. Hence, to live the indulgence of the Holy Year means to approach the Father's mercy with the certainty that his forgiveness extends to the entire life of the believer. To gain an indulgence is to experience the holiness of the Church, who bestows upon all the fruits of Christ's redemption, so that God's love and forgiveness may extend everywhere. Let us live this Jubilee intensely, begging the Father to forgive our sins and to bathe us in his merciful "indulgence."

23. There is an aspect of mercy that goes beyond the confines of the Church. It relates us to Judaism and Islam, both of which consider mercy to be one of God's most important

attributes. Israel was the first to receive this revelation which continues in history as the source of an inexhaustible richness meant to be shared with all mankind. As we have seen, the pages of the Old Testament are steeped in mercy, because they narrate the works that the Lord performed in favour of his people at the most trying moments of their history. Among the privileged names that Islam attributes to the Creator are "Merciful and Kind." This invocation is often on the lips of faithful Muslims who feel themselves accompanied and sustained by mercy in their daily weakness. They too believe that no one can place a limit on divine mercy because its doors are always open.

I trust that this Jubilee year celebrating the mercy of God will foster an encounter with these religions and with other noble religious traditions; may it open us to even more fervent dialogue so that we might know and understand one another better; may it eliminate every form of closed-mindedness and disrespect, and drive out every form of violence and discrimination.

24. My thoughts now turn to the Mother of Mercy. May the sweetness of her countenance watch over us in this Holy Year, so that all of us may rediscover the joy of God's tenderness. No one has penetrated the profound mystery of the incarnation like Mary. Her entire life was patterned after the presence of mercy made flesh. The Mother of the Crucified and Risen One has entered the sanctuary of divine mercy because she participated intimately in the mystery of His love.

Chosen to be the Mother of the Son of God, Mary, from the outset, was prepared by the love of God to be the *Ark of the Covenant* between God and man. She treasured divine mercy in her heart in perfect harmony with her Son Jesus. Her hymn of praise, sung at the threshold of the home of Elizabeth, was dedicated to the mercy of God which extends from "generation to generation" (Lk 1:50). We too were included in those prophetic words of the Virgin Mary. This will be a source of comfort and strength to us as we cross the threshold of the Holy Year to experience the fruits of divine mercy.

At the foot of the Cross, Mary, together with John, the disciple of love, witnessed the words of forgiveness spoken by Jesus. This supreme expression of mercy towards those who crucified him show us the point to which the mercy of God can reach. Mary attests that the mercy of the Son of God knows no bounds and extends to everyone, without exception. Let us address her in the words of the *Salve Regina*, a prayer ever ancient and ever new, so that she may never tire of turning her merciful eyes upon us, and make us worthy to contemplate the face of mercy, her Son Jesus.

Our prayer also extends to the saints and blessed ones who made divine mercy their mission in life. I think especially of the great apostle of mercy, Saint Faustina Kowalska. May she, who was called to enter the depths of divine mercy, intercede for us and obtain for us the grace of living and walking always according to the mercy of God and with an unwavering trust in his love.

25. I present, therefore, this Extraordinary Jubilee Year dedicated to living out in our daily lives the mercy which the Father constantly extends to all of us. In this Jubilee Year, let us allow God to surprise us. He never tires of casting open the doors of his heart and of repeating that he loves us and wants to share his love with us. The Church feels the urgent need to proclaim God's mercy. Her life is authentic and credible only when she becomes a convincing herald of mercy. She knows that her primary task, especially at a moment full of great hopes and signs of contradiction, is to introduce everyone to the great mystery of God's mercy by contemplating the face of Christ. The Church is called above all to be a credible witness to mercy, professing it and living it as the core of the revelation of Jesus Christ. From the heart of the Trinity, from the depths of the mystery of God, the great river of mercy wells up and overflows unceasingly. It is a spring that will never run dry, no matter how many

people draw from it. Every time someone is in need, he or she can approach it, because the mercy of God never ends. The profundity of the mystery surrounding it is as inexhaustible as the richness which springs up from it.

In this Jubilee Year, may the Church echo the word of God that resounds strong and clear as a message and a sign of pardon, strength, aid, and love. May she never tire of extending mercy, and be ever patient in offering compassion and comfort. May the Church become the voice of every man and woman, and repeat confidently without end: "Be mindful of your mercy, O Lord, and your steadfast love, for they have been from of old" (Ps 25:6).

Given in Rome, at Saint Peter's, on 11 April, the Vigil of the Second Sunday of Easter, or the Sunday of Divine Mercy, in the year of our Lord 2015, the third of my Pontificate.

Notes

1. Cf. Second Vatican Ecumenical Council, Dogmatic Constitution on Divine Revelation *Dei Verbum,* 4.
2. Opening Address of the Second Vatican Ecumenical Council, *Gaudet Mater Ecclesia,* 11 October 1962, 2–3.
3. Speech at the Final Public Session of the Second Vatican Ecumenical Council, 7 December 1965.
4. Cf. Second Vatican Ecumenical Council, Dogmatic Constitution on the Church *Lumen Gentium,* 16; Pastoral Constitution on the Church in the Modern World *Gaudium et Spes,* 15.
5. Saint Thomas Aquinas, *Summa Theologiae*, II-II, q. 30. a. 4.
6. XXVI Sunday in Ordinary Time. This Collect already appears in the eighth century among the euchological texts of the Gelasian Sacramentary (1198).
7. Cf. *Homily 22*: *CCL*, 122, 149–51.
8. Apostolic Exhortation *Evangelii Gaudium*, 24.
9. No. 2.
10. Saint John Paul II, Encyclical Letter *Dives in Misericordia,* 15.
11. Ibid., 13.
12. *Words of Light and Love*, 57.
13. *Homilies on the Psalms,* 76, 11.

The Embrace of Mercy

Pope Francis

"Let us never lose trust in the patience and mercy of God."

What a beautiful truth of faith this is for our lives: the mercy of God! God's love for us is so great, so deep; it is an unfailing love, one which always takes us by the hand and supports us, lifts us up and leads us on.

In today's Gospel (Jn 20:19–28), the Apostle Thomas personally experiences this mercy of God, which has a concrete face, the face of Jesus, the risen Jesus. Thomas does not believe it when the other Apostles tell him: "We have seen the Lord." It isn't enough for him that Jesus had foretold it, promised it: "On the third day I will rise." He wants to see, he wants to put his hand in the place of the nails and in Jesus' side. And how does Jesus react? With *patience*: Jesus does not abandon Thomas in his stubborn unbelief; he gives him a week's time, he does not close the door, he waits. And Thomas acknowledges his own poverty, his little faith. "My Lord and my God!": with this simple yet faith-filled invocation, he responds to Jesus' patience. He lets himself be enveloped by divine mercy; he sees it before his eyes, in the wounds of Christ's hands and feet and in his open side, and he discovers trust: he is a new man, no longer an unbeliever, but a believer.

From Pope Francis, "Homily for the Mass for the Possession of the Chair of the Bishop of Rome, 7 April 2013."

Let us also remember Peter: three times he denied Jesus, precisely when he should have been closest to him; and when he hits bottom he meets the gaze of Jesus who patiently, wordlessly, says to him: "Peter, don't be afraid of your weakness, trust in me." Peter understands, he feels the loving gaze of Jesus, and he weeps. How beautiful is this gaze of Jesus—how much tenderness is there! Brothers and sisters, let us never lose trust in the patience and mercy of God!

Let us think too of the two disciples on the way to Emmaus: their sad faces, their barren journey, their despair. But Jesus does not abandon them: he walks beside them, and not only that! Patiently he explains the Scriptures which spoke of him, and he stays to share a meal with them. This is God's way of doing things: he is not impatient like us, who often want everything all at once, even in our dealings with other people. God is patient with us because he loves us, and those who love are able to understand, to hope, to inspire confidence; they do not give up, they do not burn bridges, they are able to forgive. Let us remember this in our lives as Christians: God always waits for us, even when we have left him behind! He is never far from us, and if we return to him, he is ready to embrace us.

I am always struck when I reread the parable of the merciful Father; it impresses me because it always gives me great hope. Think of that younger son who was in the Father's house, who was loved; and yet he wants his part of the inheritance; he goes off, spends everything, hits rock bottom, where he could not be more distant from the Father, yet when he is at his lowest, he misses the warmth of the Father's house and he goes back. And the Father? Had he forgotten the son? No, never. He is there, he sees the son from afar, he was waiting for him every hour of every day, the son was always in his father's heart, even though he had left him, even though he had squandered his whole inheritance, his freedom. The Father, with patience, love, hope and mercy, had never for a second stopped thinking about him, and as soon as he sees him still far off, he runs out to meet him and embraces him with tenderness, the tenderness of God, without a word of reproach: he has returned! And that is the joy of the Father. In that embrace for his son is all this joy: he has returned! God is always waiting for us, he never grows tired. Jesus shows us this merciful patience of God so that we can regain confidence, hope—always! A great German theologian, Romano Guardini, said that God responds to our weakness by his patience, and this is the reason for our confidence, our hope (cf. *Glaubenserkenntnis*, Würzburg, 1949, p. 28). It is like a dialogue between our weakness and the patience of God, it is a dialogue that, if we do it, will grant us hope.

I would like to emphasize one other thing: God's patience has to call forth in us *the courage to return to him*, however many mistakes and sins there may be in our life. Jesus tells Thomas to put his hand in the wounds of his hands and his feet, and in his side. We too can enter into the wounds of Jesus, we can actually touch him. This happens every time that we receive the sacraments with faith. Saint Bernard, in a fine homily, says: "Through the wounds of Jesus I can suck honey from the rock and oil from the flinty rock (cf. Deut 32:13), I can taste and see the goodness of the Lord" (*On the Song of Songs*, 61:4). It is there, in the wounds of Jesus, that we are truly secure; there we encounter the boundless love of his heart. Thomas understood this. Saint Bernard goes on to ask: But what can I count on? My own merits? No, "My merit is God's mercy. I am by no means lacking merits as long as he is rich in mercy. If the mercies of the Lord are manifold, I too will abound in merits" (ibid., 5). This is important: the courage to trust in Jesus' mercy, to trust in his patience, to seek refuge always in the wounds of his love. Saint Bernard even states: "So what if my conscience gnaws at me for my many sins? 'Where sin has abounded, there grace has abounded all the more' (Rom 5:20)" (ibid.).

Maybe someone among us here is thinking: *My sin is so great, I am as far from God as the younger son in the parable, my unbelief is like that of Thomas; I don't have the courage to go back, to believe that God can welcome me and that he is waiting for me, of all people.* But God is indeed waiting for you; he asks of you only the courage to go to him. How many times in my pastoral ministry have I heard it said: "Father, I have many sins"; and I have always pleaded: "Don't be afraid, go to him, he is waiting for you, he will take care of everything." We hear many offers from the world around us; but let us take up God's offer instead: his is a caress of love. For God, we are not numbers, we are important, indeed we are the most important thing to him; even if we are sinners, we are what is closest to his heart.

Adam, after his sin, experiences shame, he feels naked, he senses the weight of what he has done; and yet God does not abandon him: if that moment of sin marks the beginning of his exile from God, there is already a promise of return, a possibility of return. God immediately asks: "Adam, where are you?" He seeks him out. Jesus took on our nakedness, he took upon himself the shame of Adam, the nakedness of his sin, in order to wash away our sin: by his wounds we have been healed. Remember what Saint Paul says: "What shall I boast of, if not my weakness, my poverty? Precisely in feeling my sinfulness, in looking at my sins, I can see and encounter God's mercy, his love, and go to him to receive forgiveness.

In my own life, I have so often seen God's merciful countenance, his patience; I have also seen so many people find the courage to enter the wounds of Jesus by saying to him: Lord, I am here, accept my poverty, hide my sin in your wounds, wash it away with your blood. And I have always seen that God did just this—he accepted them, consoled them, cleansed them, loved them.

Dear brothers and sisters, let us be enveloped by the mercy of God; let us trust in his patience, which always gives us more time. Let us find the courage to return to his house, to dwell in his loving wounds, allowing ourselves be loved by him and to encounter his mercy in the sacraments. We will feel his wonderful tenderness, we will feel his embrace, and we too will become more capable of mercy, patience, forgiveness and love.

Mercy—The Key Word of His Pontificate

WALTER KASPER

Pope Francis "says repeatedly that God's mercy is infinite; God will never tire of being merciful toward everyone if only we do not tire of asking for his mercy."

For Pope Francis, the message of mercy stands in the center of the gospel. Already as bishop, his episcopal coat of arms proclaimed the motto *Miserando et eligendo* (by gazing upon me with the eyes of his mercy, he has chosen me), following Bede the Venerable (seventh–eighth century). The topic of mercy has now become the key word of his pontificate, a topic that, from the very first day, he addresses over and over again in countless speeches. He says repeatedly that God's mercy is infinite; God will never tire of being merciful toward everyone if only we do not tire of asking for his mercy. God forsakes no person and lets none fall (*EG* 3). A little mercy among human beings can change the world.[1] With this theme he has touched the hearts of countless people inside as well as outside of the church. For who among us would not rely on a merciful God and on merciful fellow human beings?

Mercy is a central biblical theme.[2] Already in the Old Testament God is not only the God who punishes and avenges. In the revelation to Moses we hear, "YHWH is a

---

From Walter Kasper, *Pope Francis' Revolution of Tenderness and Love* (New York: Paulist Press, 2015), 31–36. Reprinted with permission.

merciful and gracious God" (Exod 34:6). The prophets and the Psalms repeat this statement time and time again: "The Lord is merciful and gracious, slow to anger and abounding in steadfast love" (Pss 103:8; 111:4). Downright dramatically, the prophet Hosea expresses the sovereignty of God in his mercy, who forgives the people and grants them a new beginning despite their infidelity: "My compassion grows warm and tender . . . for I am God and no mortal" (Hos 11:8–9).

The mercy of God is altogether pivotal in Jesus' message. Let us think only of the parable of the prodigal son, which we should better describe as the parable of the merciful father (Luke 15:11–32), or of the parable of the good Samaritan (Luke 10:25–37), or of the statement in the Letter to the Ephesians: "God, who is rich in mercy" (Eph 2:4). In addition, let us think of the Beatitudes of the Sermon on the Mount: "Blessed are the merciful" (Matt 5:7), or the statement "For I desire steadfast love [mercy] and not sacrifice" (Hos 6:6; Matt 9:13; 12:7), or Jesus' speech about the last judgment, according to which only the works of mercy count (Matt 25:31–45).

It is all the more surprising that Scholastic theology has neglected this topic and turned it into a mere subordinate theme of justice. Scholastic theology thereby has gotten tangled up in great difficulties. For when one makes justice the higher criterion, the question arises how a just God, who must punish evil and reward good, can be merciful and grant pardon. Isn't that unfair to those who have striven, in an upright manner, to live a good life?

Drawing upon Anselm of Canterbury, Thomas Aquinas was smart enough to see that God is not bound to our rules of justice. God is sovereign; he is just in relation to himself, who is love. (1 John 4:8, 16). Because God is love and therein is faithful to himself, he is also merciful. Mercy is the aspect of God's essence that is turned outward.[3] It is the fidelity of God to himself and the expression of his absolute sovereignty in love.[4]

One could also say that as God's fidelity to himself, mercy is simultaneously God's fidelity to his covenant and is his steadfast forbearance with human beings. In his mercy, God leaves no one in the lurch. Divine mercy gives everyone a new chance and grants everyone a new beginning, if he or she is eager for conversion and asks for it. Mercy is God's own justice, which does not condemn the sinner who wants to be converted, but rather makes him or her just. Let it, however, be understood: mercy justifies the sinner, not the sin. The commandment of mercy also wants the church not to make life difficult for the faithful and to make religion a form of servitude. Mercy wills—so says Thomas Aquinas, citing Augustine—that we be free of oppressive burdens (*EG* 43).[5] It is the basis for the joy that the gospel bestows (*EG* 2–8).

With this message, Pope Francis stands in the tradition of many great saints (such as Catherine of Siena, Therese de Lisieux, and others). Already for John XXIII, mercy was the most beautiful of all the divine attributes.[6] In his famous speech at the opening of the Second Vatican Council on October 11, 1962, he warned that the church today must no longer make use of the weapons of severity, but must rather apply the medicine of mercy. In this way, John XXIII already set the basic tone for; the conciliar and post-conciliar time and its new pastoral orientation.

In light of his experience of the horrors of the Second World War, the Shoah, the Nazi era, and the communist era in Poland, Pope John Paul II came to realize the message of mercy. Thus he devoted his second encyclical *Dives in misericordia* (1980) to this topic. Later he took up the suggestions of Sister Faustina Kowalska and made the Sunday after Easter Mercy Sunday. In the Jubilee Year 2000, he programmatically canonized Sister Faustina as the first saint in the new millennium.[7] Benedict XVI carried this theme forward and deepened it theologically in his first encyclical *Deus caritas est* (2005).

Pope Francis again connects originality with continuity and continuity with originality when it is a question of concrete pastoral application. He said it quite directly to the Argentine youth on July 25, 2013 in Rio de Janeiro:

> Look, read the beatitudes, which will do you good. If you then want to know what you concretely must do, read Matthew chapter 25. That is the model according to which we are judged. With these two things you have an action plan: the beatitudes and Matthew 25. You don't need to read anything else. I ask you to do this from the bottom of my heart.

Despite this unambiguous grounding in Scripture and tradition, many a person finds the pope's talk of mercy suspect: They confuse mercy with superficial laissez-faire pseudo mercy and, when they hear of mercy, they perceive the danger that what is being spoken of thereby is a weaker, pastoral permissiveness and a Christianity-lite, a way of being Christian at a reduced cost.[8] So they see in mercy a kind of "fabric softener" that undermines the dogmas and commandments and abrogates the central and fundamental meaning of truth.

That is an accusation that the Pharisees made against Jesus. Jesus' mercy so enraged them that they decided to kill him (Matt 12:1–8, 9–14). Moreover, that is a gross misunderstanding of the deep biblical sense of mercy. For mercy is itself a fundamental truth of revelation and a demanding and challenging commandment of Jesus. It stands in an inner connection with all of the other truths of revelation and commandments. Rightly understood, how is it, therefore, supposed to put into question the truth and the commandments? It also does not abolish justice, but rather surpasses it. It is the higher righteousness, without which no one can enter the kingdom of heaven (Matt 5:20). To pit mercy against the truth or against the commandments and to bring them into opposition to each other is, therefore, theologically nonsensical. In contrast, it is right to understand mercy, which is the fundamental attribute of God and the greatest of all the virtues (*EG* 37), in the sense of the hierarchy of truths as the hermeneutical principle, not to replace or to undermine doctrine and the commandments, but rather to understand and to actualize them in the right way, according to the gospel.

One can also characterize this highlighting of mercy—as a foundational hermeneutical principle—as a paradigm shift: from a deductive method to a method in the sense of see-judge-act, which begins inductively at first, and only in a second step, introduces theological criteria. Such a paradigm shift can elicit irritations and misunderstandings like the ones just mentioned, as if what had been previously said was no longer valid. However, rightly understood, the paradigm shift does not change the previously valid content of what has been taught, but certainly changes the perspective and the horizon in which it is seen and understood. Already Pope Paul VI referred to the new perspective when, in his speech during the last session of the Second Vatican Council on December 7, 1965, he described the example of the good Samaritan as the Council's model of spirituality. With this parable Jesus intends to give an answer to the question, Who is my neighbor? His answer is not deductive, but rather inductive in that it proceeds from the concrete human situation. Your neighbor is the one whom you encounter who, in a concrete situation, is in need of your help and your mercy, to whom you must bend low and bind his or her wounds. The neighbor is for you the exposition of the concrete will of God (Luke 10:25–37).

The challenge of this new paradigm stretches wide and goes deep. For if mercy is the most fundamental of all divine attributes, then through it the most fundamental of all theological questions—the question of God—is posed anew. We cannot pursue it here in this context.[9] Here we are concerned with the concrete conclusions at which Pope Francis arrives. When Jesus says, "Be merciful, just as your Father is merciful" (Luke 6:36), then that has far-reaching consequences for the shaping of Christian life through corporal and spiritual works of mercy.[10] Talk of 'God's mercy is, therefore, no pretty yet harmless cliché. It does not gently rock us in a deceptive tranquility and security; it causes us to get moving. It wants us to open our hands and, above all, open our hearts. For *misericordia* means having a heart for the poor, the poor in the widest and most comprehensive sense.

Notes

1. Pope Francis, *"Und jetzt beginnen wir diesen Weg": Die ersten Botschafter des Pontifikat* (Freiburg i. Br.: Herder, 2013), 35–38 and more often.
2. Christoph von Schönborn, *We Have Found Mercy: The Mystery of Divine Mercy* (San Francisco: Ignatius Press, 2012). Edith Olk, *Die Barmherzigkeit Gottes als zentrale Quelle des christlichen Lebens* (St. Ottilien: EOS, 2011); Walter Kasper, *Mercy: The Essence of the Gospel and the Key to Christian Life* (New York/Mahwah, NJ: Paulist Press, 2014).
3. Thomas Aquinas, *Summa theologiae* I, q. 21 a. 3 f; q. 25 a. 3 ad 3.
4. Yves Congar, "La miséricorde: Attribut souverain de Dieu," *Vie spirituelle* 106 (1962): 380–95.
5. Thomas Aquinas, *Summa theologiae* I/II q. 107 a. 4.
6. Pope John XXIII, *Journal of a Soul*, trans. Dorothy White (Garden City, NY: Image Books, 1980), 258.
7. See Hans Buob, *Die Barmherzigkeit Gottes und der Menschen: Heilmittel für Seele und Leib nach dem Tagebuch der Schwester Faustyna* (Fremdingen: UNIO, 2000).
8. See Dietrich Bonhoeffer, "Costly Grace," in *The Cost of Discipleship*, trans. R. H. Fuller, rev. ed, (New York: Macmillan, 1972), 35–47. Kasper, *Mercy*, 145–48.
9. See Kasper, *Mercy*, 84–88; bibliography on 230, n12.
10. Kasper, *Mercy*, 131–45.

II

JESUS AND THE ETHIC OF LOVE AND MERCY

Christianity and Jesus

Leonardo Boff

"The shortest and surest route to entering the reign of God is . . . to live unconditional love and unlimited mercy now."

The reign of God is not a territory, limited to the space of Palestine, but a new order of things: the last will be first, the little ones will be great; the lowly will be the masters, the sick will be healed; the deaf will hear, the oppressed will be liberated; those scattered will be reunited, suffering will disappear, mourning will be no more; death will be overcome, and the dead will arise. This program is present in [Jesus's] first public appearance in the synagogue of Nazareth (Lk 4:18–19). God will be experienced as Father of infinite mercy. The intimacy is such that he is called *"Abba,"* beloved Papa.

The reign is not just "spiritual." It encompasses all creation, and so it heals persons, feeds the hungry, halts winds, and calms the stormy sea (Mk 4:29). It forgives sins and promises grace and redemption to all, starting with those farthest away and most lost. It always preserves a character of universality and totality. No one is beyond the scope of the reign. Nothing is greater than it.

A Practice: Liberation

The dream [of the reign of God] is only true when it is translated into practice. It begins to be achieved with those

---

Excerpts reprinted from Leonardo Boff, *Christianity in a Nutshell,* trans. Philip Berryman (Maryknoll, NY: Orbis Books, 2014), 55–80.

who are last, those who are most oppressed and marginalized. Jesus comes forth as their liberator. In first place are the poor, called blessed (Mk 6:20), the privileged in the reign of God. This comes from the essence of God who, being life, feels attracted to those who have least life, because they are denied life by oppression. They are victims, the impoverished. No one is for them, they are made invisible; that is why God takes their side, comes to liberate them, and they are the first beneficiaries of the new order that is the reign of God. Then come those who are marginalized for any reason: sickness, blindness, or paralysis, or for any sort of discrimination, such as women, prostitutes, the Samaritan heretic, the publican, functionary of the empire, the Roman official, the pagan Syro-Phoenician woman, those regarded as public sinners. He eats with them, a sign that grace and intimacy with the Father also extends to them. Because of this scandalous audacity, they call him a "glutton, drinker, and friend of disreputable people" (Mt 11:19; Lk 7:34).

Full liberation is achieved in the practice of unconditional love as the organizing principle of relations among persons. Love does not divide, it unites. Even love for God goes by way of love for neighbor (Mt 23:27–40). For Jesus, neighbor means the one I come close to. And I should come close to all, but especially those that no one wants to come close to, the marginalized, the poor, the sick, and the disreputable. For Jesus, loving the neighbor means especially loving these last. "Loving those who love us, what is special about that? The evil also love those who love them" (Lk 6:32). Love for the invisible and the despised reveals the uniqueness of the love desired by Jesus, almost never practiced by Christians and the churches. In fact, unconditional love is a single movement toward the other and toward God. Jesus wants everyone to love *Abba*-Father as he has loved him, with utter trust and intimacy. Whoever has this love has everything because God himself is love (1 Jn 4:8).

But, for Jesus, love must be clothed with a quality that makes it characteristic. Love has to be merciful. Only someone who is imbued with mercy can understand and live the call of Jesus: "Love your enemies, do good to those who hate you, speak well of those who curse you, and pray for those who slander you" (Lk 6:27–28). To live this dimension of love is to be free. Offense, humiliation, and violence received keep us imprisoned in bitterness, and often with a spirit of revenge. Forgiveness frees us from these bonds, makes us fully free. Free to love. The father forgives the prodigal son (Lk 15:11–32) without demanding anything of him for his debauchery. It is not enough to be good like the obedient and faithful son who stayed home, the only one who is criticized. One must be merciful, which he was not. That is the supreme freedom: to break the chains that keep us enclosed in the past that we have suffered, and to transcend it toward the reign of freedom and autonomy. This is the work of mercy and forgiveness. Mercy is an essential quality of God: "He is kind to the ungrateful and wicked; be merciful as the Father is merciful" (Lk 6:36). Without mercy we would lose an essential dimension of the experience of Jesus toward his "*Abba*-Father, and we would be deprived of this fundamental characteristic of God. The legalists, the moralists, the authoritarians, so much a part of conservative Christian circles and in certain groups in society and civic and religious institutions, must face up to this merciful dimension of Jesus.

In the name of love he relativizes traditions, frees from oppressive laws—"the Sabbath was made for man, not man for the Sabbath" (Mt 2:27)—and subjects all power structures to rigorous critique. They cannot be for oppression, but rather must be places for exercising freedom and functions of pure service: "Whoever wants to be first must be last" (Mk 9:35).

Practice toward God goes not by way of official ritual, but by love, mercy, sense of justice, and trusting surrender to him who cares for every hair on one's head (Lk 21:18). It accepts all with no distinctions, for that is God's merciful attitude, assumed by Jesus who said: "Anyone who comes to me I will not turn away" (Jn 6:37). It may be a fearful theologian like Nicodemus, who seeks him in the dead of night, a Samaritan woman alongside the well, a blind man who cries out to him to be healed, or a desperate woman who asks him to raise up her little daughter who has just died. He attends to all without distinction. He is a being-for-others. This sentence, "Anyone who comes to me I will not turn away," expresses one of the most beautiful and emblematic of the practices of Jesus.

✦ ✦ ✦

God is *Abba*-Father because he cares for his sons and daughters, his affection rests on each of them, he knows the name that his love invented for each of them, he knows their needs, he feels their least heartbeat, he does not let a single hair of their head fall without knowing about it (Lk 21:18), he causes the sun to rise on them and the rain to fall on their heads, even when they are ungrateful and evil (cf. Lk 6:35), and he gathers them under his protection as a hen does her chicks (Mt 23:37). This *Abba*-Father shows motherly features, for he is all about care, love, and mercy, as shown in forgiveness to the prodigal son (Lk 15:11–32), in anxiety to find the lost coin (Lk 15:8–10), in the untiring search for the runaway sheep (Mt 18:12ff.; Lk 15:4). This *Abba*-Father is motherly, and this Mother is fatherly. This is the God of Jesus' root experience, God-Father-and-Mother of infinite goodness and mercy, or simply *Abba*.

✦ ✦ ✦

It is part of Jesus' message to present *Abba*-God as the Father of infinite mercy, who is remission of all debt. He asks us, "Be merciful as your Father is merciful" (Lk 6:36). Those who experience the unrestricted full mercy of the Father must live it toward those who have offended them and have acquired a moral debt toward God. That is how the "as we forgive" should be understood. It is not a negotiation with God or the establishment of a prior condition; rather, it is about maintaining the same attitude toward others that the Father has toward us. If we receive full forgiveness from God, complete remission of our debt to him, we must also give full forgiveness and complete remission to anyone who has offended us. It is a single movement, that of merciful love. How can someone who is unwilling to forgive his or her brothers and sisters receive God's forgiveness? The reign of God entails such mutuality.

✦ ✦ ✦

An Ethic: Unlimited Love and Mercy

It isn't preaching that saves but practices. This is the basic key to the ethic of Jesus. Which practices align people with the great dream of the reign of God, those that save? These practices do not sacralize, or extend, or improve existing ones. They start new ones. For new wine, new wineskins; for new music, new ears.

The first thing Jesus does in terms of ethics and behavior is free the human being. We all live behind the bars of laws, rules, prescriptions, traditions, rewards, and punishments. That is how religions and societies work; with such instruments they make people fit in, keep them submissive, create the established order. Jesus stands up to this kind of apparatus, which impedes the exercise of freedom and stifles energy: "You have heard that it was said to the ancients, but I say to you" (Mt 5:21–22). Since he is apocalyptic, he lives an ethic of urgency. Clock time is running against history. There is no halfway point: "Let your word be yes if it is yes and no if it is no" (Mt 5:37). What is most important about the law is not observing the traditions and fulfilling religious precepts, but "doing justice, mercy, and good faith" (Mt 23:23).

The essential and new thing introduced by Jesus is unconditional love. Love of neighbor and love of God are the same thing, and the meaning of all the biblical tradition is to culminate in this unity (Mt 22:37–40). The radical proposal resounds: "Love as I have loved you," which is love to the end (Jn 13:34). No one is excluded from love, not even enemies, for God loves all, even the "ungrateful and wicked" (Lk 6:35).

The law of Christ—if indeed this word "law" can be used—or rather the logic of the reign, is encapsulated in love. This love is more than a feeling and a passion. It is a decision for freedom; it is a life purpose in the sense of always opening oneself to others, letting them be, listening to them, welcoming them, and if they fall, reaching out to them. The truth of this love is tested in whether we love the vulnerable, the despised, and the invisible. It is especially of our relationship of acceptance of these wretched of the earth that Jesus is thinking when he asks us to love one another or the neighbor. Making this love the standard of moral behavior entails demanding of the human being something highly difficult and uncomfortable. It is easier to live within laws and prescriptions that anticipate and determine everything. One lives boxed in but at ease. Jesus came to tear down this inertia and to awaken human beings from this ethical slumber. He invites them, for the sake of love, to create conduct appropriate to each moment; he urges them to be alert and creative. The reign is set up whenever this loving and absolutely open and accepting stance exists. If power means anything, it is to be a potency of service. Power is only ethical if it enhances the power of the other and fosters relationships of love and cooperation among all; otherwise, the domination of some over others continues, and we become entangled in the nets of the interests in contention.

This love is expressed radically in the Sermon on the Mount. There Jesus makes a clear option for victims and for those who don't count in the present order. He declares that the blessed, that is, bearers of the divine blessings, are the poor, and that the first heirs of the reign are those who weep, the meek, those who hunger and thirst for justice, the compassionate, the pure of heart, the peacemakers, those who are persecuted for the sake of justice, those who bear insults and persecutions for the sake of the reign and put up with lies and every kind of evil (Mt 5:3–12). Indeed, the ethic of Jesus reaches even into people's innermost and hidden intentions: not only those who kill but even those who offend their brothers and sisters will be liable (Mt 5:22); even desiring another's wife suffices for committing adultery in one's heart (Mt 5:28). He states emphatically: "Do not resist the evil; if someone slaps your right cheek, offer him your left; if someone disputes with you to take your clothing, offer him your cloak as well" (Mt 5:39–40). It was such ideals of Jesus that led Thoreau, Tolstoy, Gandhi, and Dom Hélder Câmara to propose the way of active nonviolence for confronting the power of the negative.

How is this radicalism to be understood? What matters is knowing that Jesus did not come to bring a harsher law or an improved phariseeism. We will completely lose the perspective of the historic Jesus if we interpret the Sermon on the Mount and his moral indications within the framework of the law. He renders its fulfillment impossible. Or else, human beings are left in despair, as seems to have happened with Luther. What is new with Jesus is that he brings good news: it isn't the law that saves, but love, which knows no limits. There are limits to law, because its function is to create order and guarantee some harmony among people in society and to curb those who violate it. Jesus did not come simply to abolish "the law and the prophets" (Mt 5:17). He came to lay out a criterion: what comes from traditions and moral rules, if it passes through the sieve of love, will be accepted. If laws impede and hinder love, he relativizes them, as he did with the Sabbath, or he ignores them, as he did with the precept of fasting. It is love that opens up the reign. Where power prevails, the doors and windows of love, communication, solidarity, and mercy close. That applies to both society and the churches.

The supreme ideal of the ethic of Jesus is proclaimed in "Be perfect as the Father is perfect" (5:48). Jesus always emphasizes two characteristics of the Father's perfection: a love for all without barriers and an unlimited mercy. Love and mercy guide those who wish to enter the reign. It is not enough to be good and law abiding, like the brother of the prodigal son who stayed home and was faithful in all things. That is not enough. We have to be loving and merciful. Unless these attitudes are internalized, the reign does not advance, even though it is already set in motion by the practice of Jesus. When the reign is established, we will witness the great revolution in the sense of the spirit of the beatitudes: the poor will feel like citizens of the reign, those who weep will feel consoled, the nonviolent will possess and administer the earth, those who hunger and thirst for justice will see their dreams fulfilled, those who have compassion for others will experience mercy, the pure of heart will experience God directly, the peacemakers will be recognized as sons and daughters of God, those persecuted for the sake of justice will feel that they are heirs of the reign, and those who were insulted and persecuted for the sake of the dream of Jesus will be especially blessed (cf. Mt 5:3–11). Never have values been so radically reversed, as here courageously proposed by Jesus.

What is the ultimate meaning of the Sermon on the Mount, the contents of which we have just set forth and which sum up the fundamental ethic of the Jesus of history? It isn't a new law or a new ethical and moral ideal. It is something quite different. It is about establishing a criterion for measuring how far along we are on the path of the reign, near the reign or within the reign, or how far away we are, out of alignment and outside it. The Sermon on the Mount is an invitation and a challenge to us to do our utmost at this last hour, to approach the ideals that make up the content of the reign. The reign is about to break in. The colliding meteor is about to enter the earth's atmosphere and set the earth on fire. The shortest and surest route to entering the reign of God is to participate in this way in the dream of Jesus and to live unconditional love and unlimited mercy now. That is the infallible passport for entering the reign and participating in the life of the Trinity. There is no reason to fear the devastation wrought by the colliding meteor because it leads to the emergence of a new world and a transfigured humanity.

Blessed Are the Merciful

Jim Forest

"Christ is constantly ready to be merciful to anyone because he is Mercy itself."

—Jim Forest

We hand folks over to God's mercy, and show none ourselves.

—George Eliot, *Adam Bede*

But mercy is above this sceptered sway,
It is enthronèd in the hearts of kings,
It is an attribute to God himself.

—Shakespeare, *The Merchant of Venice*

Mercy within mercy within mercy.

—Thomas Merton[1]

From poverty of spirit to mourning to meekness to hungering and thirsting for righteousness. And now to the beatitude of mercy.

One of the dangers of attempting to live a righteous life is that self-righteousness is always just a breath away. How easy it is to list the sins I haven't committed, to catalogue the sins of others, to fill pages with my own good deeds. This is the situation of the righteous man whom Christ describes

---

Reprinted from Jim Forest, *The Ladder of the Beatitudes* (Maryknoll, NY: Orbis Books, 1999), 78–88.

in the parable about the Pharisee and the tax collector. The Pharisee thanked God that he was not like so many other people—thieves, cheats, adulterers—or like the tax collector in the back of the Temple. He reminded God that he fasted twice a week and gave away a tenth of his income, no small achievement then or now. Meanwhile the tax collector, overcome with awareness of his sins and his unworthiness to be in God's house or even to whisper God's name, beat his chest, begging for divine mercy (Lk 18:10–14). The tax collector's action is a seed of the Jesus Prayer: "Lord Jesus Christ, Son of God, have mercy on me, a sinner."

Christ is constantly ready to be merciful to anyone because he is Mercy itself.

One of the turning points in human history was Abraham's discovery of God's mercy when he was poised to kill Isaac, his only child. Child sacrifice was common in Abraham's world. In a cosmos controlled by easily irritated and capricious deities, the more precious the sacrificial gift, the more the god to whom it was offered might be placated—like the dragon in the medieval legend of Saint George, who was presented with maidens in order to ward off attacks on the city. Given ordinary assumptions in his world, it may be that Abraham was not astonished at the prospect of such a heartbreaking sacrifice. But at the moment when Abraham's knife was poised to shed Isaac's blood, he heard an angel say, "Abraham, Abraham." He replied, "Here I am." The angel said, "Do not lay a hand on the boy or do him any harm, for now I know that you fear God, since you have not withheld your son, your only son, from me" (Gn 22:12). Abraham, the father of the Jewish people, had approached the border of child sacrifice and been turned away from it by God's command. Jews were to be unique in the Middle East not only because they were the people of the one God, but because they did not kill their children in order to ward off God's wrath. A man raised in a culture of ruthless, blood-drenched gods had encountered the merciful God.

In our world the word "*mercy* is often used in a juridical context—a reporter might note that "the defendant threw himself on the mercy of the court." A clement judge, taking into account the particular circumstances of a crime, may decide not to punish a guilty person with the full severity of the law—a five-year sentence might be reduced by half or a person put on probation instead of behind bars.

The most commonly used Hebrew word for mercy, *khesed*, goes deeper. It can also be translated "tenderness," "kindness," "graciousness," "loving kindness," and "self-giving, unconditional love."

In the Greek New Testament the word used in the beatitude of mercy is *eleos*. We hear it in one of most repeated prayers in the Orthodox liturgy: "*Kyrie eleison*—Lord have mercy." It is linked to the Greek word *eleemosyne*: gracious deeds done for those in need, merciful giving, almsgiving. It also stands for all those inarticulate sounds associated with suffering—sighs, groans, moans, sobs, and laments.

In the Old Testament the word "mercy" is used either to describe an attribute of God—"All the paths of the Lord are mercy and truth" (Ps 25:10)—or as an appeal for God's help—"Have mercy on me, O God, in accordance with your great mercy" (Ps 51:1). Mercy is one of the divine energies revealed to all who love God, whose mercy "is infinite, reaching to the heavens" (Ps 36:5).

The Creator's mercy can rescue even those who have died: "You have delivered my soul from the depths of the grave" (Ps 86:13). This is the world Christ himself enters after his death on the cross. In the Orthodox church the most commonly displayed Paschal icon shows Christ standing on the smashed gates of hell, pulling Adam and Eve from their tombs. A text sung hundreds of times during the Paschal season rejoices that the mercy of God conquers even the grave: "Christ is risen from the dead, trampling down death by death, and upon those in the tombs bestowing life."

Mercy is central to Mary's hymn of praise for having been chosen to give birth to the Messiah:

His mercy is on them who fear him
from generation to generation. . . .
He helps his servant Israel
to remind us of his mercy,
just as he told our fathers,
Abraham and his seed, forever. (Lk 1:50, 54)

Twice in the gospels—in Matthew 9:13 and 12:7—Christ recalls the words of the prophet Hosea: "I desire mercy, not sacrifice" (Hos 6:6). He warns the scribes and Pharisees of the woe they bring upon themselves by concentrating on details of religious observance while "neglecting the weightier matters of the law: justice, mercy, and faith," thus "straining out a gnat and swallowing a camel" (Mt 23:23–24).

When those in desperate need seek his help, they cry out like the two blind men, "Have mercy on us, Son of David!" (Mt 9:27).

Christ teaches that those who seek God's mercy must pardon others. So essential is this principle that Christ includes it in the one prayer he teaches his disciples, "And forgive us our debts as we forgive our debtors." Each time we recite the Our Father, we ask the same measure of mercy from God that we give to others.

The same teaching is made even more vivid in the parable of the Good Samaritan. Asked the question, "Who is my neighbor?" Christ tells the story of a traveler whose life is saved not by two fellow Jews passing by on the other side of the road, but by a despised outsider, a Samaritan. Christ asks, "Which of the three, do you think, proved neighbor to the man who was beaten by robbers?" The man replies, "The one who showed mercy on him." Christ responds, "Go and do the same" (Lk 10:29–37).

Mercy may be essential to Christian life, yet it is far from a popular virtue. It seems more and more eroded, even in countries where Christianity is deeply rooted. In the United States, where criminal penalties in general are far more severe than in Europe, the death penalty has been reinstated in the majority of states and enjoys enormous, and passionate, public support, not least from Christians. If public hangings were resumed, it's a safe bet that they would be well attended and televised.

Still more chilling, killing by abortion and euthanasia is justified not on the straightforward grounds of convenience or economy but on claims of mercy and tenderness: we kill to end or prevent suffering. This led the novelist Flannery O'Connor to observe:

> One of the tendencies of our age is to use suffering to discredit the goodness of God, and once you have discredited his goodness, you have done with him. The Alymers [after a fictional character created by Nathaniel Hawthorne; Alymer could not bear ugliness] . . . have multiplied. Busy cutting down human imperfection, they are making headway also on the raw material of good. Ivan Karamazov cannot believe [in God], as long as one child is in torment; Camus' hero cannot accept the divinity of Christ, because of the massacre of the innocents. In this popular pity, we mark our gain in sensibility and our loss in vision. If other ages felt less, they saw more, even if they saw with the blind, prophetical, unsentimental eye of acceptance, which is to say, of faith. In the absence of this faith now, we govern by tenderness. It is a tenderness which, long since cut off from the person of Christ, is wrapped in theory. When tenderness is detached from the source of tenderness, its logical outcome is terror. It ends in forced labor camps and in the fumes of the gas chamber.[2]

Few have taken so hard and so close a look at evil as the Russian author and prison-camp survivor Alexander Solzhenitsyn. Yet Solzhenitsyn insists that the human race is not divided between the good and the evil; rather that the division is in each of us. He writes:

> The line separating good and evil passes not through states, nor between classes, nor between political parties either—but right through every human heart—and through all human hearts. This line shifts. Inside us, it oscillates with the years. And even within hearts overwhelmed by evil, one small bridgehead of good is retained. And even in the best of hearts, there remains . . . an un-uprooted small corner of evil.[3]

Not long ago I met a woman who had suddenly been made aware of that "un-uprooted corner of evil" in her own heart: Donna Eddy, a teacher in Milwaukee. We were breakfast guests of a couple we both know. Over coffee she offered to explain why she was opposed to handguns and what had made her so active with the Coalition to Abolish the Death Penalty.

While still a college student, she had a pizza-delivery job. One night her job brought her face to face with three boys who demanded the money she was carrying. Two of them had small handguns—Saturday Night Specials, she later found out.

"All I had was twenty dollars belonging to the pizza company. It wasn't my money; I didn't care, but I didn't take them seriously. Those guns looked like toys to me. As far as I was concerned, they were just kids playing a game. So I just got back in the car. Then one of the boys pointed the gun at me and started to cry. 'But I could shoot you,' he pleaded. I decided I'd better give him the money, but he didn't give me a chance. He pulled the trigger. The gun made such a little noise, just a pop, not like what you hear in the movies. I felt this hot pain, like a pellet gun.

"Thank God those boys ran as fast as they did or I would have done some terrible harm to them. I gunned the engine and used my car as a weapon, chasing after them. It took me about ninety seconds to come to my senses. I thought to myself, What are you doing? If you catch up with them, are you going to run over them?

"So I drove to the police station, but all they did was tell me I was a fool for delivering pizzas in that part of town. I still didn't realize I had been bleeding—I told the police it was just a pellet gun. But they said a medic should take a look. It was only at the hospital that I realized that I'd been shot!"

Donna was lucky. The bullet had hit her belt buckle, angled off to the side, tunneled between two layers of skin, and then come back out. It was a superficial wound but a life-changing experience. "That was the day I learned I had the potential for that kind of violence. For ninety seconds of my life, primitive rage ruled. If I'd had a gun, at least one of those boys might be dead today."

Donna Eddy's story reminded me of a turning point in the early life of a recently canonized Orthodox saint, Silouan of Mount Athos. Born in Russia in 1866, Silouan was an uneducated peasant possessing considerable physical strength and, in his youth, a hot temper. During a feast day celebrating the patron saint of his village, he was playing a concertina when two brothers, the village cobblers, began to tease him. The older of the brothers tried to snatch the concertina from Silouan and a fight broke out.

"At first I thought of giving in to the fellow," Silouan related in later life, "but then I was ashamed at how the girls would laugh at me, so I gave him a great hard blow in the chest. His body shot away and he fell backwards with a heavy thud in the middle of the road. Froth and blood trickled from his mouth. All the onlookers were horrified. So was I. 'I've killed him,' I thought, and stood rooted to the spot. For a long time the cobbler lay where he was. It was over half an hour before he could rise to his feet. With difficulty they got him home, where he was bad for a couple of months, but he didn't die."

After that, Silouan felt that there was only the slightest difference between himself and a murderer. It was only thanks to God's mercy that he hadn't killed a neighbor.

Perhaps it isn't surprising that afterward he found himself drawn to a life of prayer and penance.

After becoming a monk of Mount Athos in Greece, he thought and prayed deeply about violence and its causes. One of God's gifts to him was a profound sense of the oneness of the human race. He realized that, "through Christ's love, everyone is made an inseparable part of our own, eternal existence . . . for the Son of Man has taken within himself all mankind."

Much of Silouan's spiritual struggle centered on love of enemies, a goal that was unachievable without ardent prayer: "If we are incapable [of loving our enemies] and if we are without love, let us turn with ardent prayers to the Lord, to his Most Pure Mother, and to all the Saints, and the Lord will help us with everything, He whose love for us knows no bounds."[4]

Mercy is a hard virtue, even if it sounds like a soft quality. We want mercy for ourselves but resist extending it to others. We are eager to judge things we know little about or see from only one side. We tend to see ourselves in a good light. After all, we are more or less decent people with relatively good intentions. At least we aren't mass murderers or drug barons. But what Christ calls us to become is people living the mercy of God.

. . . For They Shall Obtain Mercy

In this beatitude the Savior speaks not only of those who show mercy by giving alms but of any form of mercy in action, for the ways of showing mercy are countless and this commandment is broad. What then is the promised reward? "For they shall obtain mercy." It seems to be a reward that equals our merciful deeds, but truly it is a far greater thing than any human act of goodness. For while they themselves show mercy as men, they obtain mercy from the God of all, and God's mercy is not the same thing as man's but is as wide as the gulf between wickedness and goodness, so far is the one of these removed from the other.

—Saint John Chrysostom[5]

For judgment is without mercy to one who has shown no mercy; yet mercy triumphs over judgment.

—Saint James (Jas 2:13)

What no eye has seen, nor ear heard, nor the heart of man conceived, what God has prepared for those who love him.

—Saint Paul Paraphrasing Isaiah (1 Cor 2:9)

At the Last Judgment the merciful receive mercy: "Come, you blessed of my Father, inherit the kingdom prepared for you since the foundation of the world. . . . Truly I say to you, whatever you did to the least person, you did to me" (Mt 25:34, 40).

While Christ cites six merciful types of activity—feeding the hungry, giving drink to the thirsty, clothing the naked, providing hospitality to the homeless, caring for the sick, and visiting the prisoner—the works of mercy include any action of caring for others, especially those who are most easily ignored, dehumanized, or made into targets of wrath rather than love. (Dorothy Day often spoke of the spiritual works of mercy: admonishing the sinner, instructing the ignorant, counseling the doubtful, comforting the sorrowful, bearing wrongs patiently, forgiving all injuries, and praying for the living and the dead.)

In a section of *The Brothers Karamazov* that echoes the Last Judgment, Dostoevsky relates the story of a woman who was almost saved by a single onion:

> Once upon a time there was a woman, and she was wicked as wicked could be, and she died. And not one good deed was left behind her. The devils took her and threw her into the lake of fire. And her guardian angel stood thinking: what good deed of hers can I remember to tell God? Then he remembered and said to God: once she pulled up an onion and gave it to a beggar woman. And God answered: now take that same onion, hold it out to her in the lake, let her take hold of it, and pull, and if you pull her out of the lake, she can go to paradise, but if the onion breaks, she can stay where she is. The angel ran to the woman and held out the onion to her: here, woman, he said, take hold of it and I'll pull. And he began pulling carefully, and had almost pulled her all the way out, when other sinners in the lake saw her being pulled out and all began holding on to her so as to be pulled out with her. But the woman was wicked as wicked could be, and she began to kick them with her feet: "It's me who's getting pulled out, not you; it's my onion, not yours." No sooner did she say it than the onion broke. And the woman fell back into the lake and is burning there to this day. And the angel wept and went away.[6]

"Hell is not to love anymore," said Georges Bernanos. It is for those who prefer not to be in communion with others. For them, to be in heaven would be worse than hell. Why would you want to be with people forever whom you have spent every day of your life on earth avoiding?

But what of heaven? When the church Fathers searched the Bible for texts that reveal what communion with God is like, they often made what seems to us a surprising choice—the Song of Solomon, a collection of love poems, many of them erotic, written to be sung at weddings: "Your love is better than wine, your anointing oils are fragrant, your name is oil poured out. . . . Arise, my love, my fair one, and come away, for lo, the winter is past. . . . My beloved is mine and I am his." Page after page celebrates the primary joy man and woman take in each other in marital love.

The church Fathers, though themselves celibate, found in this ecstatic marital poetry the best metaphor we have for God's love: human love in its most pure, unreserved, and intense form. The difference is that the love of God is infinite and absolute, while ours is temporary and limited. God's mercy is like the burning bush, which blazes but is not consumed.

Notes

1. Thomas Merton, *The Sign of Jonas* (New York: Harcourt, Brace and Co., 1953), 362.
2. Flannery O'Connor, "A Memoir of Mary Ann," pages 830–31 in *Collected Works* (New York: The Library of America, 1988).
3. Alexander Solzhenitsyn, *The Gulag Archipelago* (New York: Harper and Row, 1974), vol. 2, part 4, "The Ascent."
4. Archimandrite Sophrony, *The Monk of Mount Athos: Staretz Silouan 1866–1938*, rev. ed. (Crestwood, N.Y.: St. Vladimir's Seminary, 1973); Archimandrite Sophrony Sakharov's writings on the life of Saint Silouan, as well as the texts Staretz Silouan wrote himself, are available in a single volume, *Saint Silouan the Athonite*, published by the Monastery of Saint John the Baptist (Tolleshunt Knights by Maldon, Essex CM9 8EZ, England).
5. John Chrysostom, *Sermons on Matthew*, XV.
6. Fyodor Dostoevsky, *The Brothers Karamazov*, trans. Richard Pevear and Larissa Volokhonsky (New York: Knopf, 1990), 352.

III

A CHURCH OF MERCY

The Samaritan Church and the Principle of Mercy

Jon Sobrino

"A church of consistent mercy is the one 'marked' and 'noted in the world of today, and it is noted as a church 'according to God's command.' Consistent mercy, then, is a 'mark' of the true church of Jesus."

The theme of this monographic issue of *Sal Terrae*—"The Other Marks of the Church"—has something of the shocking about it, and much of the needful. The reference to "other marks" is shocking. Are "One, Holy, Catholic, and Apostolic" no longer enough to "mark" the true church of Jesus? And yet the topic must needs be dealt with, because these "other marks" afford us an access—a different access—to that which is fundamental: Before all else, a true church is a church "like unto Jesus." We all share the intuition that, were we to bear no resemblance to Jesus, we should not be his church, nor would that church be recognized as the church of Jesus. And so we ask: What is a church that resembles Jesus?

To resemble Jesus is to reproduce the structure of his life. In gospel terms, the structure of Jesus' life is a structure of *incarnation*, of becoming real flesh in real history. And Jesus' life is structured in function of the *fulfillment of*

Reprinted from Jon Sobrino, *The Principle of Mercy: Taking the Crucified People from the Cross,* trans. Robert R. Barr (Maryknoll, NY: Orbis Books, 1994), 15–26.

a mission—the mission of proclaiming the good news of the Reign of God, inaugurating that Reign through all signs of every sort, and denouncing the fearsome reality of the anti-Reign. The structure of Jesus' life meant *taking on the sin of the world*, and not just standing idly by looking at it from the outside. It meant taking on a sin that, today, surely, continues to manifest its greatest power in the fact that it puts millions of human beings to death. Finally, the structure of Jesus' life meant *rising again* and *raising again*—having, and bestowing on others, life, hope, and gladness.

What endows the structure of Jesus' life with its ultimate consistency can be "thought" in various ways. It can be conceptualized in terms of his fidelity, his hope, his service, and so on. Of course, none of these realities excludes any of the others. All are mutually complementary, and any of them could well serve to point up the unity of Jesus' life. What we wish to set forth in this article is that the principle that seems to us to be the most "structuring" of all, as we examine Jesus' life, is the element of *mercy* in that life. Therefore it ought to be the "most structuring" element of the life of the church, as well.

The Principle of Mercy

The term *mercy* must be correctly understood. The word has good and authentic connotations, but it can also have inadequate connotations, even dangerous ones. It suggests a sense of compassion. The danger is that it may seem to denote a sheer sentiment, without a praxis to accompany it. It may connote "works of mercy." Here the risk is that the practitioner of such works may feel exempt from the duty of analyzing the causes of the suffering that these works relieve. Mercy can connote the alleviation of individual needs but entail the risk of abandoning the transformation of structures. It may connote "parental" attitudes, but risk paternalism. In order to avoid the limitations of the concept of mercy and the misunderstandings to which it is open, we shall speak not simply of mercy, but of the principle of mercy—just as Ernst Bloch spoke not simply of hope, as if he were referring merely to one categorical reality among others, but of the hope principle.

By the principle of mercy, we understand here a specific love, which, while standing at the origin of a process, also remains present and active throughout the process, endowing it with a particular direction and shaping the various elements that compose it. We hold that this principle of mercy is the basic principle of the activity of God and Jesus, and therefore ought to be that of the activity of the church.

"In the Beginning Was Mercy"

As we know, the loving action of God stands at the origin of the salvific process. "I have witnessed the affliction of my people in Egypt and have heard their cry of complaint against their slave drivers, so I know well what they are suffering. Therefore I have come down to rescue them" (Exod. 3:7–8). The question of choosing a term to describe this activity on God's part is, in a way, a secondary one, although it would be most adequately denominated *liberation*. Our concern here is to emphasize the structure of the liberative movement. God hears the cries of a suffering people, and for that reason alone determines to undertake the liberative activity in question.[1]

We call this activity of love, thus structured, mercy. And we find that we must say of this mercy that first it is an *action*, or more precisely, a *re-action* to someone else's suffering, now interiorized within oneself—a reaction to a suffering that has come to penetrate one's own entrails and heart (in this case, the suffering of an entire people, inflicted upon them unjustly and at the basic levels of their existence). Secondly, this activity, this action, is motivated *only* by that suffering.

The interiorized suffering of another is the first principle and foundation of the reaction of mercy. But this mercy, in turn, becomes the molding principle of the whole of God's activity. After all, the mercy under consideration is not only at the origin of God's activity: It abides as a basic constant all through the Old Testament (God's partiality to victims in virtue of the sheer fact of their being victims, the active defense mounted by God in their behalf, and the liberative divine design in their regard). The mercy in question endows with their internal logic both the concrete historicization of the demand of justice and the denunciation of those who produce unjust suffering. Through this activity (and not merely on the occasion of the same), as well as through successive acts of mercy following thereon, God is genuinely revealed. The fundamental exigency for the human being, and specifically for the people of God, is that they reiterate this mercy of God's, exercising it toward others and thus rendering themselves like unto God.

Paraphrasing Scripture, we might say that, as in the absolute divine beginning "was the Word" (John 1:1), and through the Word creation arose (cf. Gen. 1:1), so mercy is in the absolute beginning of the history of salvation, and this mercy abides as a constant in God's salvific process.

Mercy according to Jesus

It is this primordial mercy of God's that appears concretely historicized in Jesus' practice and message. The *Misereor super turbas*, "My heart is moved with pity for the crowd," is more than a "regional" activity on Jesus' part. It shapes his life and mission and seals his fate. And it molds his view of God and human beings.

When Jesus wishes to show what it is to be an ideal, total human being, he narrates the parable of the good Samaritan. The moment is a solemn one in the gospels. More is at stake here than mere curiosity as to which is the greatest of the commandments: This parable is a presentation of what it is to be a human being. The ideal, total human being is represented as one who has seen someone else lying wounded in the ditch along the road, has re-acted, and has helped the victim in every way possible. The parable does not tell us what was going through the Samaritan's head at the time, or with what ultimate finality he acted. The only thing we are told is that he did what he did because he was "moved to pity."

The ideal human being, the complete human being, is the one who interiorizes, absorbs in her innards, the suffering of another—in the case of the parable, unjustly afflicted suffering—in such a way that this interiorized suffering becomes a part of her, is transformed into an internal principle, the first and the last, of her activity. Mercy, as re-action, becomes the fundamental action of the total human being. Thus, this mercy is more than just one phenomenon in human reality among many. It directly defines the human being. To be sure, mercy does not suffice to define Jesus: He is a being of knowing, hoping, and celebrating, as well. On the other hand, it is absolutely necessary that mercy come into his definition. For Jesus, to be a human being is to react with mercy. Without this reaction, the essence of the human is vitiated in its root, as occurred with the priest and the Levite who "saw him and went on."

This mercy is also the reality with which Jesus is defined in the gospels. Jesus frequently heals those who have asked him to "have pity," and he acts because he feels compassion for persons. Even God is described in terms of this mercy in another of the foundational parables. The divine Parent goes forth to meet the prodigal child, sees him, and—moved by compassion, by mercy—embraces him and declares a festival.

If the human being, Christ, and God are all described in terms of mercy, then we must be dealing with something genuinely fundamental. Of course, we may say that love is the fundamental thing, and we have the whole of Christian tradition as our warrant. That goes without saying. But we must add that the love in question here is a specific kind of love. This love is the particular *praxic* love that swells within a person at the sight of another person's unjustly inflicted suffering,[2] driving its subject to eradicate that suffering for no other reason than that it exists, and precluding any excuse for not so doing.

The elevation of this mercy to the status of a principle may seem minimal. But according to Jesus, without it, there is no humanity or divinity, and however minimal, it is genuinely maximal, as well. The important thing to observe is that this "minimum and maximum" is the first and the last. There is nothing antecedent to mercy that might move it, nor is there anything beyond mercy that might relativize it or offer an escape from it.

Simply put, this can be appreciated in the fact that the Samaritan is presented by Jesus as the consummate example of someone fulfilling the commandment of love of neighbor. But there is nothing in the account of the parable to suggest that the Samaritan succors the victim *in order* to fulfill a commandment, however lofty a one. Simply, he is "moved to pity."

We hear of Jesus that he heals people and sometimes manifests sorrow that those who have been healed have shown no gratitude. But in no wise does it appear that Jesus performs these acts of healing *in order* to receive gratitude (or in order to have it thought that he is a special person or someone with divine power). No, he performs them only "moved to pity."

Of the heavenly Parent, it is said that God welcomes the prodigal child. But there is no suggestion that this is a subtle *tactic for attaining* what God supposedly wishes (that the prodigal confess his sins and thus put his life in order). No, the Parent acts simply "moved to pity," moved to mercy.

Mercy, then, is the first thing and the last. It is more than a categorical practice of the "works of mercy." True, the practice of mercy can and ought to include these works. But mercy itself is something far more radical. Mercy is a basic attitude toward the suffering of another, whereby one reacts to eradicate that suffering for the sole reason that it exists, and in the conviction that, in this reaction to the ought-not-be of another's suffering, one's own being, without any possibility of subterfuge, hangs in the balance.

The parable exemplifies the condition of the concrete historical phenomenon as a reality shot through with mercilessness. The priest and the Levite show no mercy, and Jesus is horrified. But the evangelists are also showing us a concrete historical reality that is shaped by the active anti-mercy that wounds and kills some human beings, then kills those guided by the principle of mercy.

Because he is merciful—not a "liberal"—Jesus prioritizes the healing of the person with the withered hand over the observance of the Sabbath. His argumentation to this effect is obvious and unassailable. "Is it permitted to do a good deed on the sabbath—or an evil one? To preserve life—or destroy it?" (Mark 3:4). Nevertheless, his adversaries—described in terms strikingly antithetical to the qualities attributed to Jesus, with their "closed minds" (literally, "hardness of heart," v. 5)—not only remain unconvinced, but take action against Jesus, and the narrative concludes with these chilling words: "When the Pharisees went outside, they immediately began to plot with the Herodians how they might destroy him" (v. 6).

Notwithstanding any anachronism that may be attributed to the passage, it makes its point. It shows that mercy and anti-mercy are real. Let mercy be reduced to sentiments or sheer works of mercy, and anti-mercy will be tolerant enough. But let it be raised to the status of a principle, and the Sabbath subordinated to the extirpation of suffering, and anti-mercy will react. Tragically, Jesus is sentenced to death for practicing mercy consistently and to the last. Mercy, then, is precisely the mercy that materializes in spite of, and in opposition to, anti-mercy.

Despite the fact that his mercy is the cause of his condemnation, Jesus proclaims, "Blest are they who show mercy." The reason Jesus gives his hearers in the Gospel of Matthew could seem to fall in the category of reward: "Mercy shall be theirs" (Matt. 5:7). But the deeper reason is an intrinsic one. She who lives according to the principle of mercy realizes—renders real—the profoundest element of what it is to be human, and comes to resemble Jesus (the *true* human being of dogma) and her heavenly Parent.

Herein, we may well say, consists the blessedness, the felicity, that Jesus offers. "Blest" and happy are you "who show mercy," you "single-hearted," you "peacemakers," you who "hunger and thirst for holiness" or justice, you who are "persecuted for holiness' sake"—you "poor." Scandalous words, but enlightening. Jesus wants human beings' happiness, and the symbol of that happiness consists in their coming together at the table of sharing. But as long as the great table of the brothers and sisters of the Reign of God is missing from history, mercy must be practiced. It is mercy, Jesus is telling us, that, for the interim, produces joy, gladness, and felicity.

The Principle of Mercy

We hope these brief reflections on mercy will help the reader understand what we mean by "principle of mercy." Mercy is not the sole content of Jesus' practice, but it is mercy that stands at the origin of all that he practices; it is mercy that shapes and molds his entire life, mission, and fate. Sometimes the word *mercy* appears explicitly in the gospel accounts, and sometimes it does not. In either case, the backdrop of Jesus' activity is always the suffering of the masses, the poor, the weak, those deprived of dignity. Jesus' entrails wrench in its presence, and it is these wrenched entrails that shape all that Jesus is: his knowing, his hoping, his actions, and his celebration.

Thus, Jesus' hope is that of the poor, who have no hope and to whom he proclaims the Reign of God. His praxis is in behalf of the last and least, in behalf of the oppressed (miraculous cures, expulsion of demons, welcome of sinners, and so on). His "social theory" is guided by the principle that massive unjust suffering must be pulled up by the roots. His joy is the personal jubilation he feels when the poor understand, and his celebration is to sit down at table with the outcast. Finally, his vision of God is of a God who defends the small and is merciful to the poor. In the prayer par excellence, the Our Father, it is the poor whom Jesus invites to call God their Father.

This is not the place to expatiate on all we have just set forth. We have only meant to indicate what we have in mind, in the hope that it may help the reader understand what we mean by the "principle of mercy." This is what "informs," endows with their specific identity, all of the dimensions of the human being: knowledge, hope, celebration, and of course, praxis. Each of these dimensions has its own autonomy, but all can and ought to be molded and directed by some fundamental principle. In Jesus—as in his God—that principle, we think, is the principle of mercy.

For Jesus, mercy stands at the origin of the divine and the human. God is guided by that principle, and human beings ought to be, as well. All else is ancillary. Nor is this sheer speculative reconstruction, as is abundantly evidenced in the key passage of Matthew 25. Those who practice mercy—whatever the other dimensions of their human reality—have been saved, have arrived for good and all at the status of total human being. Judge and judged sit in the tribunal of mercy, and mercy alone. The one thing that must be added is that the criterion applied by the Judge is not an arbitrary one. Even God, we have seen, reacts with mercy to the cry of the oppressed; therefore is the life of human beings decided in virtue of their response to that cry.

Church of Mercy

It is this principle of mercy that ought to be operative in Jesus' church. And it is the *pathos* of mercy that ought to "inform" that church—give it its specificity, shape and mold it. In other words, the church, too, even *qua* church, should reread the parable of the good Samaritan and listen to it with the same rapt attention, and the same fear and trembling, with which Jesus' hearers first heard it. The church should be and do many other things, as well. But unless it is steeped—as a church at once Christian and human—in the mercy of the parable of the good Samaritan, unless the church is the good Samaritan before all else, all else will be irrelevant—and even dangerous, should it succeed in passing for its fundamental principle.

Let us notice, in function of certain key elements, how the principle of mercy informs and configures the church.

A Church "De-Centered" by Mercy

A basic problem for the church is that of determining its place with respect to the rest of reality. The formal response is a familiar one: The place of the church is in the world—in a reality logically external to it. After all, it is the practice of mercy that places the church outside itself and in a very precise locus—the place where human suffering occurs, the place where the cries of human beings resound. ("Were you there when they crucified my Lord?" sing the oppressed blacks of the United States, and their song is worth many a page of ecclesiology.) The place of the church is with the wounded one lying in the ditch along the roadside, whether or not this victim is to be found physically and geographically within intraecclesial space. The place of the church is with "the other," and with the most radical otherness of that other—his suffering—especially when that suffering is massive, cruel, and unjust.

To take its position in that place is by no means easy for the institutional church, as we are wont to call it. But neither is it easy for the merely progressive church, or for those within it who are merely progressive. Let us consider a current example. Granted, it is urgent, just, and necessary to demand respect for human rights and freedom within the church itself, especially for ethical reasons, since these human rights are signs of siblingship—signs, therefore, of the Reign of God—and because without them the church forfeits its credibility in the world of today. But let us not forget that mercy *within* the church is, in a certain sense, something secondary. With logical priority, we ought to be examining how the rights to life and liberty are faring in the *world*. This latter focus is governed by the principle of mercy and Christianizes the former; but not necessarily vice versa. Merciful Christianity can be progressive, but progressive Christianity, at times, is not merciful.

I hope I am clear about what I mean in appealing to this example. It is surely urgent for the church to become humane within. But the most important thing is that the church begin to "think itself" from without, from "along the road," where the wounded neighbor lies. It is surely urgent that the Christian, the priest, and the theologian, for example, demand their legitimate freedom in the church—a freedom so circumscribed today. But it is more urgent that they demand the freedom of the millions of human beings who do not have so much as the freedom to survive their poverty, to live in the face of oppression, or even to seek justice, be it so much as a simple investigation into the crimes of which they are the object.

When the church emerges from within itself, to set off down the road where the wounded lie, then is when it genuinely de-centers itself and thereby comes to resemble Jesus in something absolutely fundamental: Jesus did not preach himself, but offered the poor the hope of the Reign of God, grasping his fellow human beings by the lapels, giving them a shake, and urging them to the building of that Reign. In sum: It is the victim lying along the side of the road who de-centers the church and is transformed into the "other" (and the radically "other") in the eyes of the church. It is the re-action of mercy that verifies whether the church has de-centered itself, and to what extent it has done so.

Historicization of the Human Cry, Historicization of Mercy

Always and everywhere, many different classes of wounds, physical and spiritual, cry out for healing. Their size and depth vary by definition, and mercy must re-act to cure them all. However, the church must not succumb to a reckless universalization here, as if all cries expressed the same wound, or appeal to that universalization in self-justification: "We have always encouraged the works of mercy." Indeed, the church has always encouraged those works. And indeed, all human suffering merits absolute respect and calls for a response. But this does not preclude some manner of hierarchization of the wounds of today's world.

Beyond a doubt, every local church has its specific wounds, physical and spiritual alike, and all these wounds must be dressed and healed. But inasmuch as the church is one and catholic—as we say of the true church—attention must be paid to the state and condition of that wound that is the world in its totality. Quantitatively, the most painful suffering on this planet of more than five million human beings is constituted by poverty, with the death and very specific indignity that accompanies it, and that poverty remains the world's most serious wound. This deep wound appears far more radically in the Third World than in the First. Theoretically, we know all of this; still, it bears repeating. Merely by having been born in El Salvador, or Haiti, or Bangladesh, or Chad, human beings have—as Ignacio Ellacuría put it—incomparably *(muchísima)* less life, and incomparably less dignity, than persons born in the United States, Germany, or Spain. This is the fundamental wound today. And—let us recall it in Christian language—what is wounded is God's very creation.

This deepest of wounds is the deepest of wounds for any local church, not only by reason of the magnitude of the fact itself, but also by reason of the shared responsibility for it that rests with any and all local instances (governments, parties, unions, armies, universities—and churches). A local church that fails to tend that worldwide wound cannot claim to be ruled by the principle of mercy.[3]

None of this militates against the importance of tending local wounds, some of which lie along the very lines we have just sketched: those of the "Fourth World" (of the "Third World within the First") and the other specific wounds of the First World (selfish individualism and crass positivism, for example, which strip things of their meaning and persons of their faith). All of this should, of course, be tended with mercy—but without relegating to secondary status that which is primary, and without ever failing to ask oneself whether a part of the root of that absurdity, a part of the responsibility for the diseased condition of culture, might possibly be, consciously or unconsciously, our own shared responsibility in having generated a planet most of whose inhabitants bear the wound of poverty and indignity.

A Mercy Consistent to the Last

It costs the church a great deal, as it would any institution, to re-act with mercy, and it costs it even more to maintain that mercy. In theoretical terms, it is costly to the church to bow to the supremacy of the Reign of God. We frequently hear a justification of the utterly un-Christian reversal of the proper order of things—the supremacy of the Reign of God over the church—to the following effect. The very existence of the church is a great good, a boon in itself. After all, the church will, in the long run, always render the world more humane, and thus speed the coming of the Reign of God. In simple terms, we might say it is costly to maintain the supremacy of mercy over self-centeredness, and self-centeredness always becomes selfishness. Hence the temptation to which the priest and the Levite succumbed: to "see and go on." But it is especially costly to maintain the supremacy of mercy over self-interest, when, in defending the wounded victim, one finds oneself in confrontation with those forgotten players in the drama of the good Samaritan, the robbers—who also act (by re-acting).

This world is ever ready to applaud, or at least tolerate, works of mercy. What this world will not tolerate is a church molded by the principle of mercy, which leads that church to denounce robbers who victimize, to lay bare the lie that conceals oppression, and to encourage victims to win their freedom from culprits. In other words, the robbers who inhabit this anti-merciful world tolerate the tending of wounds, but not the true healing of the wounded, let alone mounting a struggle to keep the latter from falling once more into their hands.

When the church does these things, it is threatened, assaulted, and persecuted—as any institution would be. This, in turn, demonstrates that the church has let itself be ruled by the principle of mercy rather than limiting itself to the mere practice of works of mercy. Contrariwise, the absence of such threats, assaults, and persecutions demonstrates that, while the church may have managed to perform works of mercy, it has not allowed itself to be governed by the principle of mercy.

In Latin America, both phenomena are abundantly in evidence. There is a church here which practices the works of mercy but is unwilling to be governed by the principle of mercy. There is another church here that is molded by the principle of mercy, which leads it to encourage the works of mercy, to be sure, but carries it beyond them—as it carries God and Jesus beyond them. Thus, to practice mercy is to strike out at the idols, the "forgotten gods," as J. L. Sicre aptly dubs them. Forgotten does not mean vanquished. The idols of death are in hiding, but they are still very real. This is what endows with its existential ineluctability the option to maintain mercy as the first and the last, regardless of whether that will entail risks, and regardless of the type and size of these risks.

Not that we should be naive. We must realistically accept the principle of subsistency that shapes the church, as it shapes any other institution. But there are times when one must show mercy with ultimacy, and this can be done only in the presence of that which runs counter to mercy. This is what Archbishop Romero did. It was not easy for him to begin practicing this ultimate mercy, and it was even more difficult for him to maintain it. The practice of this mercy meant painful intraecclesial conflicts for him, and placed at risk his earlier ecclesial prestige, his reputation, his archiepiscopal responsibility, and his very life. It also meant risking something still more difficult to risk, and something infrequently placed at risk: the institution. In maintaining this mercy, he had to see institutional platforms of the church destroyed (the archdiocesan radio and press) and the institutional church itself decimated, through the arrest, expulsion, and murder of the most important symbols of the institution: priests, nuns, catechists, ministers of the word, and so many others. Nevertheless, Archbishop Romero held firm to the principle of mercy, and in the presence of attacks on the institution, uttered these chilling words, understandable only from the lips of one ruled by the principle of mercy: "So they have destroyed our radio, and murdered our priests? Then let them know that they have done us no harm."

When mercy is taken seriously as the first and the last, it becomes conflictive. No one is thrown in prison or persecuted simply for having practiced works of mercy. Not even Jesus would have been persecuted and put to death, had his mercy been mere mercy—without being mercy as the first and the last. But when mercy becomes the first and the last, then it subverts society's ultimate values, and society reacts.

Finally, ultimacy of mercy implies the readiness to be called a Samaritan. Nowadays the word has a positive ring. But this is because it is Jesus' name for a person of ultimate mercy. In those days, it was very pejorative, and that is precisely why Jesus used it—to emphasize the supremacy of mercy over any religious conceptions whatsoever and to attack merciless religious persons.

All this is still going on. Those who practice the mercy the robbers do not desire are called every name under the sun today. In Latin America, they are called—whether they are or not—"subversives," "communists," "liberationists," and so on. They are even murdered for it. The church of mercy, then, must be prepared to lose its reputation in the world of anti-mercy. It must be prepared to be "good," even if it is called a Samaritan for it.

The Church of Mercy Bears the Mark of the True Church of Jesus

There are many other things that can and ought to be said about a church ruled by the principle of mercy. Above all, the faith of such a church will be a faith in the God of the wounded lying along the road, the God of victims. Its liturgy will celebrate the life of the lifeless, the resurrection of One who was crucified. Its theology will be an *intellectus misericordiae (justitiae, liberationis)*, and liberation theology is nothing else. The doctrine and social practice of such a church will be a theoretical and practical obsession with indicating, and walking, effective paths to justice.[4] Its ecumenism will arise and prosper—and history shows that this is what occurs—in function of the wounded of the roadside, the crucified peoples, who, like the Crucified One, draw all things to themselves.

It is imperative, we believe, that the church allow itself to be governed by the principle of mercy. Everything that it is to be church can be organized—and in our opinion, in the most Christian manner—in function of that principle.

In conclusion, let us say three things. The first is that everything we have said up to now is nothing but a restatement, in other language, of the option for the poor that the church is obliged to make according to the declarations of the institutional church itself. Nothing that we have said is new, although it may be useful for understanding the radicality, primacy, and ultimacy of the option for the poor. The church of mercy is the one called in Latin America today the "church of the poor."

The second thing is that mercy is also a Beatitude. Therefore a church of mercy—if it really is such—is a church that feels joy because of its mercy, and therefore can show that joy. In this wise—a thing frequently entirely forgotten—the church can communicate *in actu* that its proclamation, in word and work, is *go-spel:* good news, news that is not only true, but productive of joy. A church that transmits no joy is not a church of the gospel. Of course, it is not just any random joy that must be transmitted. The church must transmit the joy declared to it in its Magna Carta, the Beatitudes, and among the Beatitudes is the Beatitude of Mercy.

The third and last thing we wish to state is that a church of mercy bears a stamp, a "mark," in the world of today. The mark of mercy stamps it, to boot, with the mark of credibility. The credibility of the church depends on various factors, and in a democratic and culturally developed world, for example, the exercise of freedom within the church and the proposal of its message in terms consistent with reason, endow it with respectability. But we believe that, in the world at large—which includes the countries of the First World—maximal credibility is a function only of consistent mercy, precisely because mercy is the thing most absent from the world today. A church of consistent mercy is at least credible. If it is not consistently merciful, it will seek credibility in vain through other means. Among those who are weary of the faith, agnostics, or unbelievers, such a church will at least render the name of God respectable. That name will not be blasphemed by the church's own actions. Among the poor of this world, the church will awaken acceptance and gratitude.

A church of consistent mercy is the one "marked" and "noted" in the world of today, and it is noted as a church "according to God's command." Consistent mercy, then, is a "mark" of the true church of Jesus.

Notes

1. In his *Teología de la liberación: Respuesta al cardenal Ratzinger* (Madrid, 1985), pp. 61ff., Juan Luis Segundo shows in detail that the finality of the Exodus is simply the liberation of a suffering people, contrary to the position of the first Vatican Instruction on the theology of liberation to the effect that the finality of the Exodus was the establishment of the people of God and the worship of the Sinai Covenant.
2. Mercy ought to be directed toward "natural" sufferings, as well. But its ultimate essence, we hold, is expressed in persons' attention to those whose suffering is precisely that of "victims." The latter, in their turn, may be the victims of either natural or historical evils, but Scripture generally ascribes far more importance to the victims of human history than to those of "natural disasters."
3. Without acrimony, and in all sibling simplicity: It is surprising that, in the last ten years of ebullient, eventful historical (and ecclesial) life in El Salvador, practically no Spanish bishop has ever paid a visit to our country and its church, with the exception of the bishop in charge of missionary work and Msgr. Alberto Iniesta, who came to Archbishop Romero's funeral at the behest and expense of his faithful of Vallecas.
4. To me, it is altogether clear that Ignacio Ellacuría allowed himself to be guided by the "mercy principle" in all his activity and specifically in his intellectual work in theology, philosophy, and political analysis. We mention this in order to emphasize that mercy is much more than either a sheer sentiment or mere merciful activism: It is also the principle of the exercise of the intelligence.

The Climate of Mercy

Thomas Merton

"The Church . . . is called to keep alive on earth this irreplaceable climate of mercy, truth, and faith in which the creative and life-giving joy of reconciliation in Christ always not only remains possible but is a continuous and ever-renewed actuality."

The mercy of God in Christ is more than forensic absolution from sin. To be called to become a new man and to participate in a new creation is, precisely, the work of mercy and not of power. Mercy is, then, not only forgiveness, but life. It is more than that. It is the epiphany of hidden truth and of God's redeeming Love for man. It is the revelation of God Himself, not as an infinite nature, as a "Supreme Being," and as ultimate, absolute power, but as Love, as Creator and Father, as Son and Savior, as Life-giving Spirit. Mercy is, then, not simply something we deduce from a previously apprehended concept of the divine Essence ("If he is the Supreme Being, then it follows that he is supremely loving, etc. . . . "), but an event in which God reveals himself to us in His redemptive love and in the great gift which is the outcome of this event: our mercy to others. Indeed, there is but one center of all mercy, one merciful event, in which we receive mercy and give it, or give it and receive it (Matthew 5:7; 6:12–14; 18:21–35). This event is the saving

---

From Thomas Merton, *Love and Living*, ed. Naomi Burton Stone and Brother Patrick Hart.

mystery of the Cross, which alone enables us to enter into a true spiritual harmony with one another, seeing one another not only in natural fellowship but in the Spirit and mercy of Christ, who emptied Himself for us and became obedient even to death (Philippians 2:2–8). The patristic theology of grace, expressed in terms of the restoration of the divine likeness to man created in the image of God and defaced by sin, must be seen in the light of this Christ-like mercy. We are "perfect as our heavenly Father is perfect," in proportion as our love is no longer restricted by a "law" or a "measure" of recognizable self-interest. If we love others only insofar as they love us, we are confined within an iron law of selfhood which seeks to assert our own existence and defend it (however hopelessly) against extinction. The love we thus give to others is the reward we offer them, the payment with which we buy their recognition of our own existence. With such love we only bribe them to help us persist in an illusion of a deathless and complete autonomy. And we bribe them by helping them defend the same illusion in themselves. But the Father makes His sun rise on the evil and the good, and our love, if we are to be sons of God, must not be limited to friends and to those who favor us or give us joy. Christian mercy falls like rain on the just and the unjust and has no law but sonship, likeness to the "perfect" Father (Matthew 5:43–48). Mercy, in other words, is at work in the freedom of the sons of God, is the full expression of that freedom, its character, its proper name, the reflection of the truth that makes us free (the truth of the merciful God revealing Himself in the eschatological event which is mercy and salvation).

To receive mercy and to give it is, then, to participate, as son of the Father, in the work of the new creation and of redemption. It is to share in the eschatological fulfillment of the work of Christ and in the establishment of the Kingdom. But without mercy, on the other hand, no zeal, no doctrine, no work, no sacrifice has in it the savor of life. It tastes of death, of *vetustas*, of the old things that have been done away with in the victory of the Risen Christ. No structure can stand that is not built on the rock of God's mercy and steadfast love *(hesed)*, and his unfailing promises.

Some English mystic of the fourteenth century has described the mercy of God in these words: "He abideth patiently, he forgiveth easily, he understandeth mercifully, he forgeteth utterly." In these simple and profound words, mercy is identified with God's knowledge of the sinner. It is not only that God looking down on the sinner as a wretched object decrees forgiveness but that He *understands mercifully*. His mercy is not merely an annulment of unpleasant facts, a refusal to see an evil that is really there. It is more: it is a seeing of the inner meaning of evil not as an entity in itself but as an incident in a saving event, as the *felix culpa* of the paschal "Exsultet." Sin is not, then, a powerful and autonomous adversary of God's mercy, one against which mercy might conceivably find itself helpless, one against which power and justice, the panoply of might and hate, ought perhaps ultimately to be displayed. God does not gaze with grim and implacable revulsion into the heart of the sinner to discern there the "thing" or the "being" which He hates. He understands the sinner mercifully, that is to say, that His look penetrates the whole being of the sinner with mercy from within so that the inmost reality of the sinner is no longer sinfulness but sonship. Then the power of mercy is free to draw the sinful existent into identity with his inmost being. Alienation is overcome. The sinful consciousness becomes capable of seeing itself face to face with the truth, without fear and without hate, because without division, the mercy of God shows the sinner to himself, no longer as existentially opposed to truth but as reconcilable with it. He becomes able to see himself as having an inner being in which truth is present. He recognizes himself as capable of a grace-filled existence, blessed by mercy, in which outward action is reconciled with inmost being. He ceases to look upon himself, whether rightly or wrongly, as a self-contradictory thing, and indeed he is absolved from the contradiction already implied by the tendency to scrutinize himself as object. This reconciliation is the ontological heart of mercy. When the sinful *Dasein* is aware of itself as understood mercifully and as "seen" full of mercy by its Creator and Redeemer, then the evil of sin, the curse of death, are "forgotten utterly." But no man can cure his own heart and deliver his own conscience from the incubus of evil merely by self-analysis and by catharsis, or merely by opening his heart to the understanding of a brother. The mercy of God must wipe out the writing that is graven in his own consciousness, and deep beneath it in the unconscious depths of his very existence. Mercy is the word of life that not only annuls the verdict of guilt but the sentence of death printed in our existence. Not that we do not die: but death itself becomes the crowning event of a saved life and the door to spirit, being, and truth in the Cross of Christ (Philippians 3:7–12).

Yet we are sinners, and we are always menaced by the dreadful power of sin, which but for God's mercy would resume its tyrannical reign in our hearts.

The alienated human existent (not fully alive to himself as being and therefore not capable of full and personal realization) requires mercy in order to get beyond the mere habit of vegetative existence. Man finds himself in the transit, the *pascha*, or passover from habitual and routine acceptance, the free and spiritual affirmation of himself as a being grounded in mercy and therefore endowed with a plenary meaning. This plenary meaning, however, takes the individual out of himself as a datum engaged in a futile struggle to endow itself with significance and plunges him into the significance with which love and mercy have saturated and irradiated man's collective being through the Resurrection of Christ.

The human existent is redeemed and delivered into the full freedom of the Christian person when it is liberated from the demonic and futile project of self-redemption—the self-contradictory and self-defeating enterprise of establishing itself in unassailable security as if its existence were identical with being, and as if it were completely autonomous. This hateful enterprise is carried on by the existent maintaining itself as "being" and as autonomous self-fulfillment, challenging and defying every other existent, seeking either to dominate or to placate all that it confronts. This implies a constant wearying effort at deception, with eager thrusts of passion and power, constantly frustrated and falling back into the cunning futility of trying to outwit reality itself.

Legal virtuousness is one of the ways in which the human existent seeks to carry out this project of deception and to gain mastery over the death that is inexorably present in the very fact of bodily life itself. There are other, more complex spiritual ways of attempting this same deception: subtle ascetic techniques, Tantric, magic, theosophical, gnostic disciplines: they are numberless, the ways in which man seeks to escape the inexorable condemnation. All are self-defeating except the Gospel mercy, in which the self-seeking self is liberated from its search and its concern, therefore to some extent from anguish, by finding not self but truth in Christ. This "finding" is the discovery, in grace and faith, that one is "mercifully understood" and that in the Spirit of this mercy and this understanding one is enabled to understand others in mercy and in pity. The weakness and defenselessness in our hearts, which make us pitiless to others, are then dispelled not by power but by trust in the divine mercy, which is given us when we no longer seek to defend our defenselessness, and are ready to accept our own boundless need in a merciful exchange with others whose poverty is as great as our own!

Man is fallen into self-contradiction and ambiguity from which no self-study, no individualistic or social ethic, no philosophy, no mere mysticism can liberate him. His Christian calling is not a calling to self-purification or to good works, to the elimination of sensual desires, to the cleansing of concepts, to the emptying of the intellect and will, to ultimate inner tranquility, and to liberation from slavery to cravings. On the contrary, his very tendency to understand the meaning of liberation in such terms may ultimately make liberation impossible.

This is a view of life, essentially "under sin," because it is under the old Law, by which Law gives sin and passion the appearance of liberty. For whenever the Law says, "Thou shalt not," there springs up in the heart of self-alienated man a doubt, and an occasion, a project of self-recovery and self-fulfillment of defiance of the Law. The promises, menaces, and demands of the Law are ambiguous because they point to self-possession and suggest two conflicting possible ways to autonomy: one by following the Law and the other by defying it. It is always possible for man under the Law, in his fallenness and confusion, to outline projects of liberty "against" the Law. But these are illusory projects which receive their apparent substance from the Law in its promises or in its threats. Thus, the Law tends to become an incitement to a despairing self-realization. It incites the self-seeking self to plunge into its own void. The very Law itself perversely and cruelly seems to define this void as "liberty" and "realization," for it tells man that he can "choose" sin and that, therefore, sinning is a form of freedom. Why this illusion? Because at the same time the Law offers a deceptive promise of fulfillment to the self-seeking self in legal righteousness. The Law is a guarantee of respectability, security, and power, and to keep the Law is to enter into the human and social structure which is founded on the Law and provides its rewards and sanctions. It is to share the power that belongs to the "elements of the world" (forgetting that they are at best "feeble elements") or even worse, perhaps, the power of the *archontes* (Ephesians 1:21). The Law offers the self-seeking self the spurious autonomy which comes from creating a place for itself in the minds of men by human righteousness and achievements: he who is justified by the Law is understood not mercifully but righteously, not by God, but by men (God says "I know you not"). He receives his reward (Matthew 6:16). This reward may be a righteous unbelief, the hardening of the heart in self-respect ("How can you believe who seek glory one from another?"). At the same time, this hardening issues in a deceptive dialogue of claims and demands with others who tend to accept this self-righteousness at its own evaluation. They accept the Law or rebel against it as it appears, incarnate in those who claim they have been justified by it.

Thus, Law without mercy kills mercy in the hearts of those who seek justification solely by socially acceptable virtuousness and by courting the favor of authority. This legal holiness, in its turn, destroys the hope of mercy in those who despair of the Law.

We must, therefore, remember the religious and Christian importance of not implicitly identifying external "Law" with interior "Mercy," either in our doctrine (and in this we usually manage to keep them distinct) or in our lives (here we tend in practice to confuse them by making the fulfillment of the Law's inexorable demand either a condition for receiving mercy or a guarantee that one has received it).

In actual fact, as St. Thomas points out, mercy and grace are the New Law—a perfect Law—binding on the Christian insofar as the other laws, in all that they have of life and meaning, are fulfilled in mercy and love. The Old Law, says St. Thomas, gave the precept of charity and mercy, but the New Law is the spring of the Holy Spirit Himself to dwell in our hearts, fulfilling Himself the command to love by giving us the power to do what was otherwise impossible (I-II, 107, 1, ad 2). "What are the (new) laws of God written in the hearts of men," Augustine asks, "if not the very presence of the Holy Spirit?" (*De Spiritu et Libera*, 21). Hence, the Law of Mercy is not an extrinsically given imperative but an inner power, not an inexorable demand imposed on a weak and confused nature but a personal inclination to love imparted by the presence of the Spirit of Sonship who makes us free, liberating us from the tyranny of natural weakness and of existential demands for self-assertion (Romans 8:2ff.).

The whole climate of the New Testament is one of liberation by mercy: liberation, through God's grace and free gift, from sin, death, and even from the Old Law. The miraculous acts of Christ in the synoptics tend generally to make this clear. The power of forgiveness is clearly associated with the power of healing and restoring to life (Mark 2:5–12). The climate of the Gospel is, then, a climate at once of mercy and of life, of forgiveness and creativity. We enter into this climate and breathe its pure air by faith, which is submission to the "New Law" of grace and forgiveness, that is to say, submission to a Law of accepting and being accepted, loving and being loved, in a personal encounter with the Lord of Life and with our brother in him. This is a "Law" in a broad and analogical sense, because it is governed not so much by fixed and abstract patterns as by the existential demands of personal love and loyalty: demands of grace and of the heart which are defined to a great extent by our own history of personal sin, need, and forgiveness. To relinquish the personal fidelity owed to Christ's grace to us in our own life, in order to return to an impersonal and abstract forensic standard, is to renounce freedom and fall back into servility and so to annul the gift of God, at the same time declaring by implication that the Cross of Christ was meaningless (Galatians 2:21). To refuse mercy is to fail in faith.

The Church, which Christ has "purchased with his blood" (Acts 2:29), is called to keep alive on earth this irreplaceable climate of mercy, truth, and faith in which the creative and life-giving joy of reconciliation in Christ always not only remains possible but is a continuous and ever-renewed actuality. This power of mercy, reconciliation, and oneness in Christ is identified with the power which raised the Lord Himself from the dead (Ephesians 1:19–20; 2:2), and vanquished the "power" of the *archontes*, the tyrannical spirits who rule "this world of darkness" and dominate over the sons of unbelief and disobedience (Ephesians 2:2). The power of mercy is the power that makes us one in Christ, destroying all divisions (Ephesians 2:14–18). Christ in His death on the Cross put an end in His own body to the conflict generated by the Law and its observances. Our access to Him is by the way of acceptance, through the mystery of the Cross (Philippians 3:9–10; Ephesians 2:16). When we enter the "fellowship of His sufferings" we receive power from God to "live together with Christ . . . in the heavenly sphere," which is the fruit of His great love, "rich in mercy" (Ephesians 2:4ff.).

But if we have received mercy, and have entered into the life of the Church in order at once to share and to proclaim the riches of mercy which make the Church the pleroma of Christ (Ephesians 1:9–12), then we must show by our mercy to others that we realize what the Christ life really means. We show that we live in the climate of creative love, the climate of the Church, to the extent that we experience the truth that it is "more blessed to give than to receive" (Acts 20:35).

Fr. M. A. Couturier (the Dominican apostle of sacred art, not the ecumenist) declared with perfect truth that many Christians "are enclosed in their Church and in their faith as others are enclosed in their Party. They aspire to a totalitarian state: and none of this has anything to do with the Gospel." In fact, the climate of totalism, which as we know to our own cost can very easily become that of religion itself, is a climate of security purchased by servile resignation under human power: obedience to the authority of might rather than freedom in the climate of life-giving love and mercy. This, of course, raises a most difficult, not to say most urgent, problem of authority in the visible structure of the Church. There must obviously be some visible authority and there must be some form of law in any institutional structure. This authority and law must be justified, as also the sacraments and the sabbath are, by being *propter homines*. They must serve only to protect and preserve the climate of mercy, or life-giving forgiveness and reconciliation. Hence, authority and power become abusive when they become ends in themselves to which the good of persons becomes subservient: when, in other words, souls for whom Christ died are allowed to be destroyed in order that power may be preserved intact.

The climate of mercy, which is the climate of the new creation, depends on the realization *that all men are acceptable before God,* since the Word was made man, dwelt among us, died on the Cross for us, rose from the dead, and is enthroned in our flesh, our humanity, in the glory of God. Hence, all that is required for a man to be acceptable before God, and a recipient of mercy, is for him to be a man and a sinner. (I did not come to call the just, but sinners . . . Matthew 9:13; Romans 5:8). We ourselves are not entitled to be more demanding than God. Whoever is acceptable to Him is, therefore, acceptable to us, and this is the test of our faith and of our obedience to Him (John 15:12, 17; 12:34–35), that we become to some extent able to be merciful to others as He has been merciful to us, knowing that this mercy is the cohesive power that establishes and manifests the Father's love in the living and unified Mystical Body of the Son (John 17:11–12, 21–22).

Hence, if a man is to be acceptable to us, nothing more is required than that he need our mercy, whether he himself is aware of this or not. It is not required that he be a certain type of man, belonging to a special race, or class, even religious customs (Galatians 5:6). Least of all is it required that he be exactly like ourselves, friendly toward us, and disposed to flatter us with a privileged consideration of our person and our ideas. The implicit demand which we formulate by asserting our own justice, setting ourselves up as a law by which to judge and evaluate other men, kills mercy in our hearts and in theirs. If I set myself up inexorably as a law to my brother, then I cannot help trying to interfere with his life by occult violence, malice, and deceit. I set myself up as a potential power to which I demand some form, be it only symbolic, of homage and submission. I set myself up, in particular, as a virtuous example which defines and identifies my brother's sin—for that in which he differs from me becomes at once "sin." Note what I do in this: I arrogate to myself a right to make him a sinner. I take to myself the awful power which Paul ascribed to the law, of bringing to life sin in my fellow man (Romans 7:8–10). Nor is this power illusory. It is most real and most malevolent in strong collective groups whose ideologies can create a bad conscience and even a sense of guilt and self-hate in supposedly "lesser breeds without the law." We have seen this force at work in colonialism and in racism, where the arrogance of unscrupulous and self-righteous power has deeply wounded the consciousness of millions of men. From these deep wounds will spring new "laws" of violence, hatred, and revenge.

In the climate which is not that of life and mercy, but of death and condemnation, the personal and collective guilts of men and of groups wrestle with one another in death struggle. Men, tribes, nations, sects, parties set themselves up in forms of existence which are mutual accusations. They thus seek survival and self-affirmation by living demonically, for the demon is the "accuser of the brethren." A demonic existence is one which insistently diagnoses what it cannot cure, what it has no desire to cure, what it seeks only to bring to full potency in order that it may cause the death of its victim. Yet this is the temptation which besets the sin-ridden *Dasein* of man, for whom a resentful existence implies the need and the decision to accuse and to condemn all other existences. Note here the peril of the tyrannical concept of God as a mere limited "existent" among other existents. Such a God becomes a tribal totem, a magnification of the self-seeking existent striving to establish its autonomy in its own void. Can such a God be anything but the embodiment of resentments, hatreds, and dreads? It is in the presence of such idols that vindictive and death-dealing orthodoxies flourish. These gods of party and sect, race and nation, are necessarily the gods of war.

There is a false and demonic mercy, then, which grows in the soil of this kind of accusing existence, an existence forfeit to self-complacency and contempt, an existence rooted in resentment, hatred, and war. Such mercy, having (let us suppose) successfully awakened guilt in the other, absolves the guilt when sufficient gestures of submission have been extorted from him by force or manipulation. But it is not Christian mercy to create a bad conscience in my brother and then entice him by pardon into my own poisoned bosom, admitting him into the stifling climate of my own lovelessness.

This demonic falsification of mercy constitutes one of the most serious religious problems of our era. Indeed, the whole future of the Christian missionary apostolate is hanging on the solution of the ambiguities that have arisen from this. The solution cannot even be guessed at until the problem itself is faced, and the times are forcing us to face it. It is the problem of the inevitable and often perfectly sincere confusion that once identified the Gospel with Christian and Western cultural values. The bitter truth of Auschwitz and Hiroshima has begun, it seems, to clarify this situation. Even to the blindest among us, the confusion is beginning to be evident.

One fruit of this evidence is that the mercy which we often think we are bringing to men is less merciful than we believed, and that it is we, in fact, who most need to receive mercy from those to whom we have preached it. The grace of the word preached to Africa is perhaps the paradoxical realization of our own sin, our own need to be pardoned, and in particular our immense need to be pardoned by Africa.

Made in the context of an essay honoring Albert Schweitzer, such a statement might seem to be either unnecessarily romantic or simply out of place. At any rate, he better than any other would be able to say if there is truth in it. The grace of his particular vocation is a grace of solitude and uniqueness. Neither solitude nor uniqueness is ever comfortable: there is always the risk that such isolation might be prophetic, fraught with prophetic silence and doubts, moments of self-questioning abandonment and of dread. One's very isolation may seem an accusation of others who are "not there" and others in turn who are not there may take occasion, from the unique case of a Schweitzer, to justify their absence and their inertia. On the shoulder of this one man, and of perhaps a handful of others like him, has fallen the whole burden of white Christendom. Such a burden is not only a responsibility but even a temptation, a temptation which the rest of us must thank him for facing. His vocation (a monk may be permitted to say this) is in the most authentic monastic tradition of *peregrinatio*, exile, solitude, and love. We must not forget that works of mercy were combined with solitude not only in the ideal of Basilian monachism but in that of Syria, Egypt, and of the Benedictine West. It is such uncompromising sacrifice and renunciation that confer upon the monk the right to perform good works that have a monastic and charismatic dimension, not reducible to the mere official ministrations of the paid functionary, however dedicated he may be.

At no time can the mystery of mercy be understood if we become obsessed with finding out who is the creditor and who is the debtor. The climate of mercy becomes life-giving and creative when men realize that they are all debtors, and that the debt is unpayable. (St. Anselm, who is too often accused of having fabricated a completely legalistic soteriology, was actually making this point clear.) Only in the Cross are all debts paid, and there are no solutions between man and man, or man and God, that can fully satisfy the claims of mercy and redemptive, reconciling love as if they were the demands of commutative justice. The claims of mercy are demands in a totally new sense: demands not that the debt be properly measured and then generously paid, but that *the whole root of indebtedness* be laid open to the light that "understandeth mercifully" and thus seen to be quite other than we thought. There can be no question of a limit to pardon—a pardon that becomes meaningless and ineffectual after "seven times" (Matthew 18:21). We seek that divine mercy which, enduring forever (Psalms 106:1), and dynamically active as a leaven in history, has entirely changed the aspect of human existence, delivering it from its forfeiture to a syndrome of accusation, projection, resentment, and ultimate despair. We seek it not only in our hearts and minds but in man's world, his common life on earth.

Mercy heals in every way. It heals bodies, spirits, society, and history. It is the only force that can truly heal and save. It is the force that has been brought into the world in the great eschatological event of the Cross, in order that man might be totally renewed, and that the guilt-ridden and despairing *Dasein* of the lost human person might find itself reconciled in freedom and mercy with the needs and destinies of others and of the world itself. Mercy heals the root of life by curing our existence of the self-devouring despair which projects its own evil upon the other as a demand and an accusation.

When we are enabled by God's gift to become merciful, we are given the power to understand mercifully, to accept and to pardon the evil in others, not as a fruit of some godlike magnanimity rooted in our own justice, but first of all as the fruit of a self-knowledge which is liberated from the need to project its own evil upon the other.

After this, when we have learned not to see an evil which is perhaps not there in any case, we become able to see the same evil in ourselves, to accept it, to repent of it, and (knowing that we are understood mercifully) to forget utterly. The work of mercy is this understanding and this forgetfulness.

"The characters which accompany wealth," said Aristotle, "are plain for all to see. The wealthy are insolent and arrogant, being mentally affected by the acquisition of wealth, for they seem to think that they possess all good things; for wealth is a kind of standard of value of everything else so that everything seems purchasable by it." This is true not merely of individuals but of societies as well. The true "Law" of our day is the law of wealth and material power. The fate of men, indeed of mankind itself, depends on the laws of economics. It is the market that in reality determines the existence, indeed the survival, of all men and dictates the ideals and the actualities of social life. In our time the struggle of mercy is, then, not against rigid and inflexible morality but against a different and more subtle hardening of heart, a general loss of trust and of love that is rooted in greed and belief in money. What irony that this faith in money, this trust in the laws of the market, this love of wealth and power, should have come to be identified with Christianity and freedom in so many minds, as if the freedom to make money were the freedom of the sons of God, and as if (Bloy pointed this out) money had demonically usurped the role in modern society which the Holy Spirit is supposed to have in the Church.

The love of power and gain becomes the demonic pseudo-pneuma which leads men and institutions, ostensibly "Christian," to trample on the hearts of their fellow men, to destroy primitive social structures which had a semblance of equity, beauty, and order, leaving in their place nothing but slums built out of gasoline cans and ultimate degradation. Obedience to this "spirit" and to the social values which it inspires, whether in marketing nations or in totalistic societies, is servitude to an inhuman banality that is blind to the most elementary human instincts and insensitive to the most fundamental contacts (the infinitely banal "sanity" of an Eichmann, and the hideous caricature which was his "obedience"!). Our whole future, the very survival of humanity, appears mortgaged and closed by this demonic legalism, this blasphemous caricature of "order."

Can the power of evangelical mercy possibly break through this iron ring of satanic determinism? We must believe that it can, or else we are not fully Christians. But our optimism must not be utopian and sentimental. Obviously a mercy that is confined to the dimensions of individual piety can at best illuminate our abdication with a warm, sentimental glow. Today it is not enough for a few individuals to be kind, to understand, and to pardon. This can too easily become a sheer mystification, particularly if it seems to absolve everyone else from serious responsibility in social life.

Though there is no use placing our hopes on a totally utopian new world in which everyone is sublimely merciful, we are obliged as Christians to seek some way of giving the mercy and the compassion of Christ a social, even a political, dimension. The eschatological function of mercy, we repeat, is to prepare the Christian transformation of the world, and to usher in the Kingdom of God. This Kingdom is manifestly "not of this world" (all forms of millennial and messianic Christian optimism to the contrary), but it demands to be typified and prepared by such forms of heroic social witness that make Christian mercy plain and evident in the world.

But in a world of huge atomic stockpiles, a Christian mercy that confines itself to interior feelings of benevolence and "good intentions" in the use of appalling destructive power can manifestly not meet the demands of eschatological love. The only event that can be ushered in by this kind of sentimentality is too grim to be contemplated, and it belongs more to Antichrist than to the Kingdom of the risen Kyrios.

Christian mercy must discover, in faith, in the Spirit, a power strong enough to initiate the transformation of the world into a realm of understanding, unity, and relative peace, where men, nations, and societies are willing to make the enormous sacrifices required if they are to communicate intelligibly with one another, understand one another, cooperate with one another in feeding the hungry millions and in building a world of peace.

Such is the eschatological climate of the new creation, in which pardon replaces sacrifice (Osee 6:6; Matthew 9:13) and the whole world is filled with the mercy of God as the waters cover the sea.

IV

THE WORKS OF MERCY

The Corporal Works of Mercy and the Spiritual Works of Mercy

JAMES F. KEENAN, S.J.

"Mercy is above *all the experience we have of God."*

The Corporal Works of Mercy

As the willingness to enter into the chaos of another, mercy best conveys the actions of God who creates by bringing order out of chaos and who redeems by lifting us out of the chaos of sin. Christ's own entrance into the chaos of death occasions our hope in the risen life. His pledge to return is a pledge to deliver us from the chaos of our own lives. Mercy is above all the experience we have of God.

In response to that mercy, we become imitators of the God in whose image we are made. And so, in answer to Christ's call to follow him, we practice mercy. The centrality of the practice of mercy in the life of the church cannot be overlooked. It ranks among the activities that best describe the moral life: the confessing of one's sins, obeying the Ten Commandments, developing the virtues, and practicing the corporal and spiritual works of mercy.

Much could be written about how the corporal works of mercy developed as such. We know them to be seven: feed

---

From James F. Keenan, S.J., *The Works of Mercy: The Heart of Catholicism* (Lanham, MD: Rowman and Littlefield, 2005), 9–13, 61–64. Reprinted with permission from Rowman and Littlefield.

the hungry, give drink to the thirsty, shelter the homeless, clothe the naked, visit the sick, visit the imprisoned, and bury the dead. These are later paired with the spiritual works: give good counsel, teach the ignorant, admonish sinners, console the afflicted, pardon offenses and injuries, bear offenses patiently, and pray for the living and the dead.

While the first six of the corporal works of mercy are found in the Last Judgment parable in Matthew 25:34–45, it took several centuries for the final articulation of these seven to become a cornerstone of the Christian life. Eventually they parallel other groups of seven, such as the seven sacraments, the seven deadly sins, and the virtues (four cardinal; three theological).

The Early Church Promotes the Works of Mercy

Before the set mantra of seven was firmly situated, Christians heard the divine injunction to practice mercy. John never tires of recommending it (1 John 4:20–21, for example). Luke tells us how deacons are appointed to serve the most marginalized (Acts 6:1–6). Paul writes to Timothy about the selection of widows who, like the deacons, are to serve those in need (1 Timothy 5:9–10). Collectively and institutionally the apostolic church promotes the service of mercy.

Almsgiving becomes a near expression of mercy. Clement writes, "Almsgiving is good as a penance for sin; fasting is better than prayer, but almsgiving is better than both, and charity covers a multitude of sins" (2 Clement 16). In the apostolic age, the practice of mercy is expressed in taking up a collection on the first day of every week (presumably during the Eucharist) as Paul instructs the Corinthians (1 Corinthians 16:1–2).

These many calls to mercy are heeded. For instance, Cyprian, bishop of Carthage, leads his congregation to respond to victims of the plague in 252. Bishop Dionysius provides a narrative of his community's response to the plague in Alexandria in 259. "Most of our brethren, in their surpassing charity and brotherly love did not spare themselves and clinging to one another fearlessly visited the sick and ministered to them. Many, after having nursed and consoled the sick, contracted the illness and cheerfully departed this life. The best of our brethren died in this way, some priests and deacons, and some of the laity" (Eusebius, *Hist. Eccl.* 7.22.9).

Why is the call to mercy made? Normally six motives are found in the writings of the Scriptures and among the fathers.

- First, Proverbs 15:27 encourages us to practice mercy for the remission of our sins, that is, in gratitude for God's merciful stance toward our sinfulness. John Chrysostom sees mercy, in this passage, as the queen of the virtues, outweighing all our burdensome sins.
- Second, Tobit 12:8–9 tells us that for our prayers to be heard by God, works of mercy should accompany them. Several of the fathers, Augustine, Cyprian, Leo the Great, and John Chrysostom, preach on this theme.
- Third, Matthew 6:20 suggests that works of mercy will lead to eternal reward, a motivation that Augustine often uses.
- Fourth, no less than Matthew 25:40 reveals to us that any merciful action is for the sake of the Lord. Cyprian calls this the most powerful of all motives. Here, many of the fathers promote the figures of Mary of Bethany and Zacchaeus as models of mercy. Similarly, the celebrated episode of Martin of Tours giving his cloak to the beggar becomes a motif throughout the church.
- Fifth, Lactantius and Ambrose urge mercy to fortify human solidarity and to extend the circle of fellowship in the Lord.
- Finally, Clement of Alexandria, John Chrysostom, and Leo the Great remind us that works of mercy bring

us into the life of perfection. By practicing mercy we become more like the God who entered into our own chaos.

The Middle Ages and the Renaissance

In the Middle Ages, the monasteries become centers for extraordinary mercy. One account from the famed monastery at Cluny, for instance, informs us that seventeen thousand persons are cared for in one year. Among the Cistercians, every abbey has a guest house for pilgrims, travelers, and the poor where the abbot waits on them, after first welcoming them by prostrating himself at their feet.

Besides the monks, pious laypersons participate in the works of mercy by forming "lay associations." These begin in Naples in the tenth century and later appear in Tuscany. By the twelfth century they are throughout France, Spain, and Italy, assisting members of religious orders in their apostolates mostly by establishing and maintaining hospitals. For instance, in 1217, a hospital that once belonged to a religious community is handed over to a corporation of four priests, thirty laymen, and twenty-five laywomen. By the thirteenth and fourteenth century these activities are flourishing throughout Europe.

With the spirit of Francis and Dominic in the thirteenth century, many professional laypersons become inspired and answer the call to mercy with great imagination. For instance, in 1244, the head porter of a wool guild in Florence (Pier Luca Borsi) forms the Company of Mercy with money collected by taxing colleagues for swearing. Others reach out to those suffering from leprosy. The Knights of St. Lazarus alone established three thousand hospitals for those suffering from the dreaded disease. Later hospitals for the blind and foundlings for orphans are also founded.

One effect of the Crusades is the widespread practice of prostitution. In its aftermath, foundations are established to provide sanctuaries to the women; in turn, the women form religious congregations. In the thirteenth century, for instance, the Congregation of the Penitents of St. Mary Magdalen has thirty communities throughout Europe.

By the sixteenth century, the establishment of guilds along with the innovations of new religious orders like the Jesuits, as well as the important reforms of the Council of Trent, provide new impetus for laypersons to belong to confraternities, the successor of "lay associations." In the next, seven chapters I shall examine these confraternities, which wedded spiritual growth and devotion with the practice of mercy. Here I mention only two. The Company of Divine Love is established to respond to those with syphilis, which breaks out throughout Europe in the mid-1490s. Sufferers from this incurable disease are abandoned both by families because of shame and by hospitals because of fear of contagion. In 1499 the first hospital for the incurables is built in Genoa, then another in Rome, and others in Naples, Venice, and finally throughout Europe. The company heralded the continent's response of compassion to those afflicted by the awful disease.

In 1498 Queen Eleanor of Portugal establishes the Confraternity of Misericordia. In 1516 it has one hundred members: fifty from the nobility, fifty from the working class, all dedicated to the fourteen works of mercy. By the queen's death in 1525 there are sixty-one branches of the confraternity. From the seventeenth to the nineteenth century, twenty-five confraternities are established in Portuguese colonies. Many still stand today.

We cannot underestimate the relevance of these confraternities: Hundreds of them take care of prisoners and captives; others are established for the care of the mentally ill as well as those who are unable to hear and/or speak. These confraternities are only paralleled by the extraordinary number of religious orders which themselves adopt a work of mercy to identify with their own charism.

Conclusion

Today many persons speak of the emerging lay ministry. But during a variety of periods in the church's life, laypersons—animated both by their own God-given talents and by the fundamental experience of God's mercy—were ministers. Their legacy of leadership and service needs to be studied, for it was phenomenal. A proper place to find it is in the variety of lay associations and confraternities in both the medieval and Renaissance periods. In those times of spiritual richness and economic prosperity, times like our own, the laity, alongside clergy and religious, imitated the merciful ways of the Good Samaritan.

✦ ✦ ✦

The Spiritual Works of Mercy

Like the corporal works of mercy, the spiritual works are seven: instruct the ignorant, counsel the doubtful, comfort the afflicted, admonish the sinner, forgive offenses, bear wrongs patiently, and pray for the living and the dead. While the corporal works call Christians to respond to those with specific needs that are lacking—shelter, food, water, clothing, and so on—the spiritual works are a little more complicated. On the one hand, like the corporal works, the first three deal with spiritual burdens that the neighbor suffers: the ignorant who lacks instruction in faith and morals, the doubtful who lacks the certitude of faith and morals, and the afflicted who experiences life's burdens not only corporally but also spiritually. The next three deal with matters of strife and reconciliation. They are appeals to the Christian to take significant steps toward maintaining the harmony of the community rife with many problems. In that sense the "spiritual" building-up is the reconciler herself, the one who admonishes, forgives, and bears wrongs. Certainly there is a spiritual building-up of the sinner, the forgiven, and the wrongdoer, but these three spiritual practices particularly redound to the reconciler and the community itself. By bearing wrongs patiently, the reconciler grows in virtue. Finally, the last spiritual work, the call to pray, builds up the entire community, both through the one who prays and through the one for whom the practitioner prays.

While the beneficiary of the corporal works is the recipient, it is the reverse among the spiritual works: Often the beneficiary is the one who practices the spiritual works.

Unlike the corporal works, the spiritual works were first recommended to individuals. We saw a strong corporate legacy to each of the corporal works of mercy. Often an early diocese, a medieval religious order, a thirteenth-century lay association, or a Renaissance confraternity decided on a corporal task: ransoming the prisoner, sheltering the homeless, feeding the hungry. With the exception of the instruction of the ignorant, most of the spiritual works were not appropriated corporately but rather personally. There were no confraternities known for bearing wrongs patiently or forgiving offenses, however, nor were religious orders counseling the doubtful or admonishing sinners. Moreover, the calls to comfort the afflicted and pray for the living and the dead were so general that, unlike the corporal works, neither religious orders nor confraternities could assume them as specific charisms. Thus the spiritual works are proposed in a very general way to each and every Christian. They are not works looking for specific groups to assume them, but invitations to individual Christians to practice them.

Certainly, monasteries, religious orders, lay associations, and confraternities did practice these within their own communal identities. We can easily recall the famed chapter rooms, where individual monks knelt at the center of their communities and received the admonition of community members. But again, these were practices for the building-up of the individual and the community and were not charisms specific to a particular community the way the corporal works were.

Looking Back to Understand the Spiritual Works

The spiritual works developed in both Eastern and Western Christianity during patristic times. Origen recognized that Matthew 25 was not only a call to dress the body with clothes or to feed it with food, but also a summons to tend to the spiritual needs of the other. In many ways the roots of the call came through the appreciation of the Christian as being one—body and soul.

In the early literature the original corporal works had spiritual counterparts: the spiritually hungry, naked, thirsty, and so on. Moreover, inasmuch as Christians frequently sought to privilege the state of the soul over the state of the body, preachers from Origen through John Chrysostom warned listeners to attend not only to their siblings in need of physical nourishment, but also those in need of the word of God.

Such concerns were often accompanied by another set of issues. The epistles urged Christians to pardon, give mutual support, and exhort each other (as in Ephesians 4:32 and Colossians 3:13, 16). These biblical recommendations too were looking for a home in the emerging tradition of the church. Indeed, in 2 Corinthians 5, Paul urges his readers to become ambassadors of reconciliation, imitating the very action of God in reconciling the world. If the Christian is the follower of Christ the incarnate one, then the Christian is called to do what Christ did: reconcile.

This call to reconciliation, along with the call to be vigilant about the spiritual needs of the other, eventually coalesced into the spiritual works of mercy. The long-standing development through the tradition finds a comparable occurrence in the writings of Augustine. Around 378 in *De moribus ecclesiae catholicae*, Augustine describes a hodgepodge of concerns. But by 421, when he writes the *Enchiridion*, he proposes the corporal works of mercy and adds a few: console the afflicted, show the way to the lost, assist those who hesitate. Spiritual invitations to be mindful of other disciples on the way of the Lord are sensitive to the "weaker" sibling. They invite one to become the spiritual caregiver of others: building up oneself, one's weaker brother or sister, and the community as a whole. After proposing these three, Augustine offers a second form of "almsgiving": pardoning. In his sensitivity, Augustine sees the full picture, that pardoning is not only forgiving sins and bearing wrongs, but includes correcting and rebuking the sinner; this too is mercy (chapter 72).

Augustine then turns to the greatest of all alms: forgiving debtors and loving enemies. The one who has practiced the other works will bc better able to realize this most challenging of all Christian tasks. For it is easy to do good to those who have done us no harm, but to forgive from the heart those who have harmed us is the real challenge of the Gospel. Augustine realizes that the challenge is fraught with difficulties and informs us that before we look to the great task of loving our enemy, we need to call on the Lord to have mercy on us. We need to recognize our own need for spiritual mercy. It is here, among the spiritual works of mercy, that we see Augustine's interest in promoting the love of self as he reminds the Christian to give alms first to her or his own self:

> For the one who wishes to give alms as he ought, should begin with himself, and give to himself first. For almsgiving is a work of mercy; and most truly is it said, "To have mercy on thy soul is pleasing to God." And for this end are we born again, that we should be pleasing to God, who is justly displeased with that which we brought with us when we were born. This is our first alms, which we give to ourselves when, through the mercy of a pitying God, we find that we are ourselves wretched, and confess the justice of His judgment by which we are made wretched, of which thc apostle says, "The judgment was by one to condemnation"; and praise the greatness of His love, of which the same

> preacher of grace says, "God commends God's love toward us, in that, while we were yet sinners, Christ died for us"; and thus judging truly of our own misery, and loving God with the love which He has Himself bestowed, we lead a holy and virtuous life. (chapter 76)

For Augustine, the works of mercy are very much a way for the Christian to acknowledge God's mercy. They bring the work of salvation full circle, helping the Christian to see the gift of mercy, which enables us to practice the task of mercy.

Finally, it is after Augustine that the seventh spiritual work, all-encompassing prayer for the living and the dead, emerges. Here, this third form of almsgiving, as it is named, is first conveyed as a general, but deeply felt well wishing for all people including one's enemies. The third form of spiritual almsgiving is a summary of all the foregoing.

The Scandal of the Works of Mercy

DOROTHY DAY

"It is by the works of mercy that we shall be judged."

The Spiritual Works of Mercy are: to admonish the sinner, to instruct the ignorant, to counsel the doubtful, to comfort the sorrowful, to bear wrongs patiently, to forgive all injuries, and to pray for the living and the dead.

The Corporal Works are to feed the hungry, to give drink to the thirsty, to clothe the naked, to ransom the captive, to harbor the harborless, to visit the sick, and to bury the dead.

When Peter Maurin talked about the necessity of practicing the Works of Mercy, he meant all of them. He envisioned Houses of Hospitality in poor parishes in every city of the country, where these precepts of Our Lord could be put into effect. He pointed out that we have turned to state responsibility through home relief, social legislation, and social security, that we no longer practice personal responsibility, but are repeating the words of the first murderer, "Am I my brother's keeper?"

The Works of Mercy are a wonderful stimulus to our growth in faith as well as love. Our faith is taxed to the utmost and so grows through this strain put upon it. It is pruned again and again, and springs up bearing much

---

From Dorothy Day, "The Scandal of the Works of Mercy." *Commonweal*, November 4, 1949.

fruit. For anyone starting to live literally the words of the Fathers of the Church—"The bread you retain belongs to the hungry, the dress you lock up is the property of the naked"; "What is superfluous for one's need is to be regarded as plunder if one retains it for one's self"—there is always a trial ahead. "Our faith, more precious than gold, must be tried as though by fire."

Here is a letter we received today: "I took a gentleman seemingly in need of spiritual and temporal guidance into my home on a Sunday afternoon. Let him have a nap on my bed, went through the want ads with him, made coffee and sandwiches for him, and when he left, I found my wallet had gone also."

I can only say that the saints would only bow their heads and not try to understand or judge. They received no thanks—well, then, God had to repay them. They forbore to judge, and it was as though they took off their cloak besides their coat to give away. This is expecting heroic charity, of course. But these things happen for our discouragement, for our testing. We are sowing the seeds of love, and we are not living in the harvest time. We must love to the point of folly, and we are indeed fools, as Our Lord Himself was who died for such a one as this. We lay down our lives, too, when we have performed so painfully thankless an act, for our correspondent is poor in this world's goods. It is agony to go through such bitter experiences, because we all want to love, we desire with a great longing to love our fellows, and our hearts are often crushed at such rejections. But, as a Carmelite nun said to me last week, "It is the crushed heart which is the soft heart, the tender heart."

Such an experience is crueler than that of our young men in Baltimore who were arrested for running a disorderly house, i.e., our St. Anthony's House of Hospitality, and who spent a few nights in jail. Such an experience is even crueler than that which happened to one of our men here in New York who was attacked (for his pacifism) by a maniac with a knife. Actually to shed one's blood is a less bitter experience.

Well, our friend has suffered from his experience and it is part of the bitterness of the poor, who cheat each other, who exploit each other even as they are exploited, who despise each other even as they are despised.

And is it to be expected that virtue and destitution should go together? No, as John Cogley has written; they are the destitute in every way, destitute of this world's goods, destitute of honor, of gratitude, of love; they need so much that we cannot take the Works of Mercy apart and say: I will do this one or that one Work of Mercy. We find they all go together.

Some years ago there was an article in *The Commonweal* by Georges Bernanos. He ended it on a warning note for these apocalyptic times:

> "Every particle of Christ's divine charity is today more precious for your security—for your security, I say—than all the atom bombs in all the stockpiles."

It is by the Works of Mercy that we shall be judged.

What Is the Place of the Spiritual Works of Mercy in Our Life Together?

SIDNEY CALLAHAN

"None of the spiritual works of mercy come with ready-made patterns to follow."

We belong to a social species whose members depend upon human bonds and attachments to survive and flourish. Humans must love and care for each other but are imperfectly prepared to do so. Because human weaknesses and sin are always present, and because of the disordered world in which we find ourselves, every human being needs others. Christians affirm that our human response to life should be to love God with our whole heart and mind, and our neighbor as our self. Theologians now make it clear that love of God and love of neighbor are essentially one and the same, for God is in each of His creatures as well as transcendently beyond all imagining. In Scripture Christ tells us that what we do for the least of our fellow human beings we do for him. From these Gospel injunctions to love and work toward God's kingdom, the Church articulated the traditional teachings on the works of mercy.

From Sidney Callahan, *With All Our Heart and Mind: The Spiritual Works of Mercy in a Psychological Age* (New York: Crossroad, 1988), 14–19. Reprinted with permission from Sidney Callahan.

The works of mercy are a Christian's response to God's love; they are love in action. In grateful imitation of God's love and mercy to us, Christians attempt to "be merciful as your Father in heaven is merciful." Of course there is a vast difference in what humans can do compared to God's love and power, but we are still called to do what we can. As wounded imperfect persons we do not do works of mercy as though we possess all good things in abundance and dispense them at will. A Lady Bountiful distributing turkeys, baskets of cheer, and instruction is the wrong image. A spiritual or personal psychological work of mercy is not simply a matter of giving things that we have to those without. It must be a very different process. Central to understanding this process is a grasp of the idea that thoughts, prayers, emotions, speech, or goodwill are not really "things" but are essentially personal actions. Acts directed to other self-conscious persons are enacted in a dynamic interrelationship that affects us as we act. In consciousness-to-consciousness communication we change as we reach out to one another. Understanding this mutuality I can quite humbly undertake things that would be inappropriate and arrogant if viewed as a one-way directive or gift from a superior to an inferior.

Fortunately, modern psychologists have come up with an old but new-sounding concept of "the wounded healer." Who can better understand and help another person than one who has suffered the same weakness or can empathetically experience it. In modern forms of personal mediation, those who have recovered from an addiction, those who have been in prison, and those who have been through other crises are acknowledged as those most able to help the similarly afflicted: "I can understand you, I have been there." The incarnational principle that those who have lived through a situation can best help others justifies the Christian efforts to offer help. Every Christian conscious of sin, personal suffering, and the need to be healed can try to meet another's need.

The spiritual or psychological works of mercy are necessary because we have all experienced suffering and the brokenness of life to a certain degree. Who has not sinned, doubted; been ignorant, or hurt? We have all been there, and can respond in love to our fellow beings when they suffer or lose their way. As wounded healers we can reach out to others with humility whatever our stage of spiritual development. Fortunately, we do not have to have reached the illuminated way, or have experienced mystical heights to engage in these ordinary enterprises of daily life among ordinary people. All of us can reconsider and reflect on what these spiritual or self-giving efforts will mean today. And of course there will be different times in our lives when certain works of mercy or ways of loving are more appropriate than others.

Life as we lead it, whether stumbling along or purposefully marching to meet goals, has a way of presenting us with unexpected challenges. Fervent youth may champ at the bit seeking heroic challenge and sacrifices. Older pilgrims know that what turns up will be hard enough. The great Saint Teresa had youthful visions of herself going off to martyrdom among the Moors, but she found dealing with the pettiness and inertia of the people at home enough of a challenge. My own observation has been that everyone, regardless of vocation or goals, eventually experiences a well-rounded spiritual curriculum. Nuns or married women, priests or fathers of families, professionals or peasants, every temperament and intellect seems to need and to receive specifically tailored tutoring to learn to love God and neighbor. These varied experiences cannot all happen at the same time, of course, so persons look as though they are on much more distinct ventures than may really be the case. When we see someone whose life seems spiritually easy, so smoothly flowing, so untroubled by temptation or struggle, I think that we should remember that every life is lived in stages over time. We do not know what has already been struggled with or what may yet come, and our outsider's perspective is very different from a person's inner experience. The same can also be true of lives that outwardly seem unbearably crushed by misfortune, although we should not for this reason feel indifferent or apathetic toward the suffering of others.

God is definitely a God of surprises. New experiences and challenges, both joyful and excruciating, can occur in even the most routine life. In my experience, those who seek God are never bored or becalmed for long. Most of us will never reach those spiritual depths where the saints suffered extended dark nights of the soul. But the testimony seems to be that, even for them, periods of dryness finally pass and give way to new times of growth. Periods of jogging along uneventfully seem relatively brief. Just as we think we have mastered some stage or challenge in life, it changes. Unexpected joys may suddenly come: C. S. Lewis entitled his autobiography *Surprised by Joy*, and he was wise to do so; long after he wrote his book he found new love and a late marriage with a woman named Joy. But it is also true that we can be caught off guard by some particular suffering we could not imagine ever having to confront. After his unexpected idyllic marriage, C. S. Lewis had to suffer the early death of his wife, with all the agonies he could hardly have foreseen in his days as a self-sufficient Oxford don.

Like Lewis and everyone else, I too have experienced more joyful things in life than I could ever have dreamed were coming. And like others, I have also experienced suffering and traumas that were total shocks from out of the blue: the sudden death of a parent, a child, an emergency operation, a devastating betrayal of love. In the human condition a person can be catapulted from a totally joyful condition in which all is happiness to the deepest grief: sorrow, and anxiety. In my life unexpected sufferings and crises produced a complete reliance upon God and responsive spiritual acts of mercy on the part of my friends. God rescues us out of the depths of misery and friends offer support. Spiritual assistance is less dramatic, but still present in the more slowly developing problems of life that produce chronic suffering:

the alienation of a child, problems with alcoholism or disease, struggles with work, or financial problems.

While joys and grace abound, life is also hard. We all need to help and be helped as we struggle on. The great novelist Henry James has his characters ask their friends in moments of stress, "Will you see me through?"—through illness, betrayal, or the task of overcoming evil. So, too, all of us who attempt to lead a Christian life need others to see us through: The spiritual works of mercy are ways that we do this for one another. All such psychological efforts require energy. God makes such expenditures of energy possible, and occasionally even easy to do, but often we have to work against our natural inertia and laziness. It is so much easier not to get involved; the slang, expression "Who needs it?" sums up our natural resistance to becoming enmeshed with others when we would just as soon retreat.

Listening to the Church's demand for love and works of mercy spurs us on. Within the tradition of the Church the range of the corporal and spiritual works of mercy serves as a corrective to our penchant for designing a narrower Christian life. Just as the unexpected joys, opportunities, and sufferings that come our way push us in undreamed of directions, so the breadth of the works of mercy challenges us to expand and expend ourselves. All of these different ways of expressing charity will challenge us at different times and in different situations. Naturally, some actions will be more difficult for us than others; the great struggle in the self's interaction with others is getting things into balance and proportion.

In fact, if one type of action is too easy for us we might be suspicious of our motivation. Am I always, for example, too eager to admonish the sinner, or too ready to weep with the bereaved? Or is it always easier for me to bear wrongs patiently than risk conflict by admonishing the sinner? In God, justice and mercy are joined, but we find it difficult to discern ways to practice both. None of the spiritual acts of mercy come with ready-made patterns to follow.

V

LIVING MERCY

Divine Mercy—
The Audacity of Mercy

Joan Chittister, O.S.B.

"To be without mercy is to be yet without an honest awareness of our own humanity."

Thomas Ann Hines, a divorced mother of an only child, learned mercy the hard way. When her son, a freshman at college, lay murdered by a seventeen-year-old drifter who first solicited a ride from him and then, when he got in the car, turned a gun on the young driver, Thomas Ann descended into a pit of anger and vengeance. The murder was a random, groundless, indefensible act. And her son was not the only person who died that night—Thomas Ann was alone, distraught, full of the kind of pain and hate that paralyzes the heart and stops life in its tracks, even for the living.

Her son, a good boy, a successful student, the hope of her life, was gone. She herself was completely alone now, without a future, without hope, without any reason, it seemed, to live.

But thirteen years later, Thomas Ann Hines visited her son's killer in prison, intent only on getting information about the night of the killing. But when, in the course of the conversation the young man put his face down on the

---

From Joan Chittister, O.S.B., *God's Tender Mercy: Reflections on Forgiveness* (New London, CT: Twenty-Third Publications, 2010), 8–18. Reprinted with permission.

small table at which they sat and began to sob, she touched the man. And she got to know him.

The story shocked the country. "How could she do such a thing?" people asked. Or, more to the point, perhaps, they asked themselves the question, "Could I ever do such a thing? Could I possibly show mercy to someone who had done something so senseless, so heinous, so destructive to me?"

Thomas Ann's answer to the question was a simple one: "If my son was sitting in this room" she said, "I'd want someone to reach out a hand and lift him up."

The story is not only a moving one, it is an enlightening one for all of us. It teaches us something very important about mercy. Mercy is what God does for us. Mercy discounts the economic sense of love and faith and care for a person and lives out of a divine sense of love instead. Mercy gives a human being who does not "deserve" love, love. And why? Because, the Scriptures answer, God knows of what we are made.

The fact is that we are all made of the same thing: clay, the dust of the earth, the frail, fragile, shapeless thing from which we come and to which we will all return someday. We are all capable of the same things. Our only hope is that when we are all sitting somewhere bereft, exposed, outcast, humiliated and rejected by the rest of society, someone, somewhere will "reach out a hand and lift us up."

Every one of us is capable of every sinful thing. Most of us have simply never had the opportunity or the anger or the sense of desolation it takes to do it. While we're being grateful for that, it behooves us to be merciful to those who have.

Mercy is my answer to my own weaknesses. When those weaknesses erupt in me, may those around me remember their own. "If you wish to receive mercy," St. John Chrysostom wrote, "show mercy to your neighbor."

The mercy and understanding I show to others is the degree of mercy, the kind of understanding I will get when I need it most.

To be without mercy is to be yet without an honest awareness of our own humanity.

It is one thing to be righteous; it is another thing to be merciful. Righteousness only confirms us in our pride. Mercy is a sign of humility.

Mercy is what enables us to raise law above the stringency of legalism to the ultimate level of human idealism. "Mercy," Thomas Aquinas wrote, "is the fulfillment of justice, not its abolition."

When we understand why people do things, we have the capacity to change life for the better at its very roots.

To thirst for the punishment of another is to abandon ourselves to the kind of standards we know down deep we cannot keep.

We pray for mercy, we expect mercy. What we find difficult to do is to be merciful to those in need of it. Or as George Eliot says, "We hand folks over to God's mercy, and show none ourselves."

The great spiritual question is not whether or not this person, this situation deserves mercy. It is about whether or not we ourselves are capable of showing it.

The major holy-making moment in our own lives may be when we receive the mercy we know we do not deserve. Then, we may never again substitute disdain for understanding, rejection for openness, legalism for justice. "I think perhaps it is a better world," Helen Waddell writes, "if one has a broken heart. Then one is quick to recognize it, elsewhere."

Learning to withhold judgment is difficult in a media-driven world but essential in a better one. "Forgiveness," Christian Baldwin writes, "is the act of admitting we are like other people."

Mercy is learned first in the human heart. "If you haven't forgiven yourself something," Dolores Huerta writes, "how can you forgive others?"

Not uncommonly, those who are self-righteous are most sinful themselves. Because they hate themselves for what they are, they can't possibly be merciful to anyone else.

Because history shows us that the church is a sinful church, it is the very place in which we should be able to find the greatest degree of mercy, of understanding, of compassion, of non-judgmentalism.

To be merciful is to be kind, to be open, to be trusting, to be a friend. Mercy, Shakespeare writes, "is twice blest. It blesseth him that gives and him that takes." It is when we show mercy that we may be closest to God.

Mercy is what makes us, keeps us, available to one another. It opens our heart to strangers. It enables hospitality. It is the glue of the human race. Tennessee Williams understood the relationship of mercy to human interdependence when he wrote, "I have always depended on the kindness of strangers."

Coming to understand that there is nothing unforgivable in life is the beginning of real love.

Mercy is the trait of those who realize their own weakness enough to be kind to those who are struggling with theirs. It is, as well, the measure of the God-life in us. "The weak," Gandhi wrote, "can never forgive. Forgiveness is the attribute of the strong."

Beware those who show no mercy. They are dangerous people because they have either not faced themselves or are lying to themselves about what they find there.

"We are all sinners," we say, and then smile the words away. But the essayist Montaigne was clear about it: "There is no one so good," he wrote, "who, were they to submit all their thoughts and actions to the laws, would not deserve hanging ten times in life."

It is our very weaknesses that enable us to understand the power, the necessity of mercy.

The Sufi mystic Mishkat al-Masabaih reminds us, when we are overwhelmed by our own inadequacies, our own diversions from the straight paths of life, that the mercy of God is always greater than the sin of being too humanly human. He writes: "She who approaches near to Me one span, I will approach near to her one cubit; and she who approaches near to Me one cubit, I will approach near to her one fathom; and whoever approaches Me walking, I will come to her running; and she who meets Me with sins equivalent to the whole world, I will greet her with forgiveness equal to it."

The mercy we show to others is what assures us that we do not need to worry about being perfect ourselves. All we really need to do is to make the effort to be the best we can be, knowing we will often fail. Then, the mercy of others, the mercy of God is certain for us, as well. "The only thing we can offer to God of value," St. Catherine of Sienna said, "is to give our love to people as unworthy of it as we are of God's love."

To hold others to standards higher than our standards for ourselves is to live in constant agitation, personal, national, and global. "Unless it extends the circle of its compassion to all living things," Michael Nagler writes, "humanity will not itself find peace."

To become "God-like" is the most common—and the most elusive—of all spiritual aspirations. What can that injunction—that desire—possibly mean? A medieval mystic answers the question directly. "When are we like God?" the mystic Mechthild of Magdeburg writes. "I will tell you. Insofar as we love compassion and practice it steadfastly, to that extent, do we resemble the heavenly Creator who practices these things ceaselessly in us."

When we, too, "know of what were made," there is no room in us for anything but mercy for the other. "Being all fashioned of the self-same dust," Longfellow wrote, "let us be merciful as well as just."

Mercy takes us outside ourselves. It makes us one with the rest of the world. Or as Martin Luther King, Jr., reminds us, "The first question which the priest and the Levite asked was, 'If I stop to help this man, what will happen to me?' But the Good Samaritan reversed the question. He said: 'If I don't stop to help this man, what will happen to him?'"

A sign in Springdale, Connecticut, makes the whole subject clear. It reads: "There is so much good in the worst of us and so much bad in the best of us, that it's rather hard to tell which of us ought to reform the rest of us."

Strange, isn't it? We expect that God will show us mercy; but, too often, we show so little ourselves. We believe fiercely in capital punishment; we tolerate the thought of nuclear war; we suspect whatever is unlike ourselves. If heaven is based on the same punitive, violent, and segregating principles, we are all in trouble.

The strangest of all human phenomena, perhaps, is that we take God's mercy for granted for ourselves but find it so hard to be merciful ourselves. If there were any proof needed that God is completely "Other," this is surely it.

> Perhaps forgiveness is the last thing mentioned in the Creed because it is the last thing learned in life. Perhaps none of us can understand the forgiveness of God until we ourselves have learned to forgive. Perhaps we cannot understand the goodness of God to us because we are so seldom that good to others.
>
> On the contrary, we want mercy for ourselves but exact justice for the remainder of humankind. God, on the other hand, the Creed implies, desires justice but gives mercy like a rushing river, gushes mercy like a running stream. (Joan Chittister, *In Search of Belief*)

"It is often the most wicked who know the nearest path to the shrine," the Japanese proverb reminds us. Don't let anybody fool you: Goodness is as goodness does. Be careful who you call bad simply because the "good" people have named them so. God, it seems, is far less quick to judge.

Living in the Mercy

ELAINE M. PREVALLET, S.L.

"Mercy makes our hearts spacious; it also mercies the space around us. Mercy becomes the space we live in."

Recently I was in a doctor's office waiting for an appointment when a young mother with long brown hair and a gentle face entered, pushing in a wheelchair a child three or four years old. The child obviously was disabled: her hands unable to grasp anything, her arms and legs flailing helplessly, her eyes unable to hold focus. Her voice could not make syllables but only squeals or little wails. The mother positioned the child's chair so that they were face-to-face. She began softly singing and doing the hand motions to "The Itsy Bitsy Spider" directly in front of the child's face, to attract her attention. She repeated it over and over, sometimes catching the child's hand and kissing it, stroking her hair; she looked into the child's eyes and whispered, with enormous tenderness, "I love you." For a moment, I felt like an unwitting intruder into a sacred space.

Is this how we are, I wondered, before our God who wants to love us just this tenderly? Our limbs flailing aimlessly, unable to unify our energies to respond to the gift of life we have been given; our eyes unable to focus on the love God tries over and over in so many ways to reveal to us; our voices unable to respond coherently to this God whom our

---

From Elaine M. Prevallet, S.L., "Living in the Mercy," *Weavings* 15/5 (September-October 2000): 6–13. Reprinted with permission from Elaine M. Prevallet.

minds cannot comprehend? And is that why we so often turn to the word *mercy* when we want to speak of our God?

When God's love touches us in our neediness, the sorrow and suffering inherent in the human condition, we name it mercy. Mercy is perhaps the loveliest of all God's qualities. This is the love that reaches into the dark space of our flailing and our failing, our losing and our dying. Mercy enters that space, picks us up and holds us tenderly until we are healed. Little by little, this love draws our groping hands and wasted energies to purposeful service; it looks directly into our uncomprehending eyes, hears our futile wail, and says, *No matter. I love you anyway. Come on. . . .* And so mercy brings us to ever-new life.

Mercied by God

The concept of a merciful God is found in many ancient texts. In the Hebrew scriptures, worshippers are reminded that God's mercy (or steadfast love) endures forever (Ps. 118; Sir. 51). Several Hebrew words are translated by the English word mercy, especially the word *rahamim*, derived from the word for uterus *(rehem)*. Even though attributed to male gods, mercy is most like womb love, the deeply bonded, intimate, often prescient love of a mother for her child who has, for the first nine months of its life, shared the mother's body space (Isa. 49:14–15). Mercy creates a sort of ambience, and spatial metaphors seem peculiarly congenial for expressing its special quality.

For Dame Julian of Norwich, fourteenth-century English anchorite and mystic, mercy was at the very heart of God. When she speaks of God's relationship to us, Julian often uses spatial, womb-like images, suggesting a mutual indwelling. We are "enclosed" in the Father, the Son, and the Spirit, she says, even as the holy Trinity is enclosed in us (Ch. 54).[1] God is "our clothing, who wraps and enfolds us for love, embraces and shelters us, surrounds us for his love" (Ch. 5). "Our Lord Jesus, comely and tall and full of honour," she says, sits in the midst of our heart, "his home of homes and his everlasting dwelling" (Ch. 68). Julian consistently uses such spatial images to convey her deep sense of God's encompassing, safe, accepting Love.

Julian speaks in boldly paradoxical terms of Jesus as carrying us within himself as a mother carries a child: "Our savior is our true Mother, in whom we are endlessly born and out of whom we shall never come" (Ch. 57). In his "motherhood of mercy and grace, . . . our precious Mother Jesus" feeds us with himself, most courteously and tenderly, with the blessed sacrament (Ch. 60). Throughout our lives he is guiding, protecting, teaching, strengthening, nourishing, and never leaving us. "The sweet gracious hands of our Mother are ready and diligent about us," acting as a kind nurse attending to the safety of her child (Ch. 61). Such feminine images consistently act as the lens through which Julian sees God and our relation to God. The space around us, as well as within us, is completely "mercied" by God's loving care; we are endlessly "oned" to God in love. "Our life is all founded and rooted in love, and without love we cannot live" (Ch. 49).

Julian saw our sinfulness and our burdens, but saw also that God keeps us as tenderly and sweetly when we are burdened as when we are consoled. "In falling and in rising we are always preciously protected in one love" (Ch. 82). Regardless of how miserable we feel or how hard on ourselves we may be, there is no moment in our lives when God is not holding us in love. We are at all times safely enclosed in mercying love: we live *in* the Mercy.

Why is it so difficult for us to allow that to be true? Julian's experience with a multitude of humanity alerted her to some perennial ways that we, in our sinfulness, can obstruct God's love. Perhaps surprisingly, the two kinds of sin that Julian believed most "belabor and assail us" and that our Lord desires should "be amended," are first, "impatience and sloth," and second, "despair or doubtful fear" (Ch. 73). She seems to mean by this that we have a tendency to bear our troubles heavily and to grow weary and discouraged; and in addition we make ourselves wretched going over and over how awful and unworthy we are. Though Julian is surely aware of the human potential for heinous sin, her focus on these internal attitudes is interesting. It must reflect her concern for the ordinary good people who came to her window for counsel and comfort. She knew they were well intentioned, they were trying hard to do their best to please God—probably not unlike ourselves. There was no need for them to feel more fear or worthlessness than they already did. Her words, I believe, are directed to the dailyness of their reality—and to ours.

For many of us, perhaps particularly women, discouragement and self-doubt are regular and familiar inhabitants of our inner space, wearyingly able to keep us trapped in feelings of worthlessness and fear. Here, then, is need for the mercy. God "shows us our sins by the sweet light of mercy and grace" (Ch. 40), and "wishes that we forget our sin with regard to our unreasonable depression and doubtful fears" (Ch. 73). We fall into that despondency, Julian believes, simply because of our "ignorance of love" (Ch. 73). But, in a process undergirded by mercy, our very self-blaming wears us out, and so opens us to realize how distrusting we are in the face of God's steady, tender love. "Our courteous Lord," as Julian calls him, "does not want his servants to despair because they fall often and grievously; for our falling does not hinder him in loving us" (Ch. 39). We cannot escape experiences of failure and pain: they are simply facts of life. But God tells Julian not to waste time blaming herself, as if such experiences were all her fault. God doesn't want her to be "immoderately depressed or sorrowful" (Ch. 77). These feelings of inadequacy and failure are the dark space into which mercy enters, enabling us to carry our troubles and illnesses, our failures and humiliations, to consciously suffer them, resisting what needs to be resisted, accepting what cannot be changed. We may regard them, Julian says, as "penances"—and surely these penances are tailor-made for us, and much more effective than the ones we choose for ourselves!

Rather than being depressed and pushed down by our failures, then, or magnifying and rehearsing them over and over, Julian would have us remember the mercy, and turn ourselves over in trust to the God whose mercying love is ever-present and unchanging. This is the wise advice of a seasoned guide of souls whose own heart is securely grounded in the mercy of God.

These thoughts of Julian can help us ponder our own inner space. Is it peopled with voices that accuse or threaten us, that make us fearful and guilty, that criticize and belittle us? Do we hang on to our humiliations, rehearsing the scenarios, and so keep ourselves paralyzed by them? Do we give space to voices that continually demean and judge others, in a subtle but futile effort to shore up our own adequacy? Only as we become aware of such voices or attitudes and determine to hold them—and ourselves with them—in the Mercy, can we be internally freed from them. Mercying love, accepting us as we are, allows us also to accept ourselves with our limitations, but not to allow them to claim ownership of us. We begin to shift focus from our failings to God's mercy, and we are gently led to understand that our failings do not inhibit mercy but rather summon its healing power. In addition, we ordinarily find ourselves much more tolerant of the failings of others. We begin to *live* in the Mercy.

In our prayer, we can hold ourselves in the mercy of God, and ask to be delivered from our obsession with our failures. We refocus; we can imagine ourselves surrounded by an all-encompassing love, sense ourselves "wound with mercy round and round as if with air."[2] More than all the striving we may do to perfect ourselves, this inner attitude of receptivity sets us on track. There is deep security and comfort in this sense of being surrounded by a great and accepting love, living in the Mercy.

What kind of space do we create *around* ourselves? Just as inner peace and contentment create a certain ambience around us, so does internal prickliness. Internal attitudes of harsh judgment either upon ourselves or upon others make us prickly; they indicate that defenses are up, that entry into our heart space will encounter thorny obstacles. Their effect is that people will almost automatically feel on their guard in our presence. If we really believed that we were surrounded by love, and if we were to entrust ourselves to that love, we would instinctively and effortlessly provide gracious, warm, and comfortable space around us that is ready to receive and welcome persons as they are. A kind of spaciousness would characterize us, both individually and collectively, allowing a person to be free to be herself; subtly eliciting what is best from another, allowing her to "flower from within." Mercy makes our hearts spacious; it also mercies the space around us. Mercy becomes the space we live in.

Entering the Wounded Place

What can all this say to the everyday world we inhabit, in which safe space is increasingly a rare commodity? Children are taught early on never to trust strangers. Fathers and mothers—invoked as images of divine love—can be abusers. Violence, oppression, injustice, poverty, war—a whole catalog of outrageous evils make such inward-turned reflection sound like pious pap, totally irrelevant to the so-called *real world.* How does mercy reach into the social fabric—or does it?

Julian's visions of God's mercying love are not all sweetness. She saw in graphic detail the blood flowing from the body of Jesus as he was scourged. Jesus' blood was "precious" and "plentiful," and it overflowed all the earth, ready to wash clean from sin all creatures (Ch. 12). Here is a powerful symbol of compassionate love, a love willing to suffer, pouring itself out so copiously that it reaches everywhere in the universe that Julian knew—the lower regions of hell, all the way up to heaven. Julian sees the *whole* of creation united in the suffering of Christ—what we would now call solidarity: "I saw a great unity between Christ and us . . . for when he was in pain we were in pain, and all creatures able to suffer pain suffered with him" (Ch. 18).

The blood of Christ encloses the whole creation in the mercying love of God, continually at work bringing life out of death. Further, Julian repeatedly emphasizes that it is through his pierced side that Jesus draws us into the divine life: "With a kindly countenance our good Lord looked into his side, and he gazed with joy, and with his sweet regard he drew his creature's understanding into his side by the same wound; and there he revealed a fair and delectable place, large enough for all mankind that will be saved . . . " (Ch. 24). The words *kindly, joy, fair and delectable place* should not deflect our attention from the central metaphor: entrance into the life of God, the place of salvation, the space in which mercy is at work, is through the scourged and wounded body of Christ. The metaphor seems to insist that it is by sharing in—entering into—the suffering, the brokenness, the wounds of humanity that we share in the life of God. And not just our own brokenness. Julian's vision comes back again and again to our oneness in Christ, our solidarity with each other and with all creation.

Our hearts either expand and deepen or they shrivel. They expand as we embrace the whole of life, resisting suffering (our own and others') that should not or need not be and accepting what cannot be avoided—both attitudes turned toward the service of Life. Our hearts shrivel as we cut ourselves off in an effort to avoid the pain of the paschal process, the process of cross and resurrection in which we glimpse the hope that all suffering can issue in new life. We will not be saved—we will not enter into life with God—except through that one portal of the wounded side of Christ, the space in which we are in solidarity with the rest of creation, dying together and rising together into new life. That is the space where Mercy lives.

How do we enter this space? Paradoxically, we enter the brokenness of Christ by allowing it to enter us. Jesus shared broken bread with his disciples, saying. "Take, eat; this is my body" (Matt. 26:26, NSRV). New life comes through our capacity to ingest that very brokenness. This is the central fact of life. Therefore, mercy is not a weak or sentimental love. It sees things as they are, sees the cruelty, the pain, looks the brokenness right in the face, takes it all in. Then mercy draws us to recognize our solidarity with any part of creation that is suffering, oppressed, handicapped, or victimized. It moves us, as it moved Jesus, to act with love and integrity, at whatever cost, to do whatever the situation requires of us to resist, expose, advocate, remedy. Jesus is God's firm promise to be present in all of our reality, always intent upon bringing life out of death. In Jesus, we know that God's love is, relentlessly, mercy.

With Mercy Wound About

Surely, in the end, after all our righteous judgments on what is wrong with ourselves, each other, and with the world; after we experience injustice intractably resistant to our most devoted efforts, leaving us with our thirst unquenched, our mouths dry and our throats sore from protest; surely in the end the gospel calls us to view the whole of creation, and each other, with the eyes of mercy, and to love it all anyway, with a mercying heart.

In the haunting ending of Archibald MacLeish's play, *J.B.*, after everything has been lost, Job's wife, Sarah, is sitting on a doorsill holding a broken twig of forsythia. "Look, Job," she says; "this forsythia, the first few . . . petals . . . I found it growing in the ashes, gold as though it did not know. . . . You wanted justice and there was none—only love."

Job: "He does not love. He Is."

Sarah: "But we do. That's the wonder."

Admitting that she had contemplated suicide, she says, "Oh, I never could! Even the forsythia . . . " (She is half laughing, half crying.) "Even the forsythia could stop me." They cling to each other, peering at the darkness inside the door. Job says, "It's too dark to see." And Sarah responds, "Then blow on the coal of the heart, my darling. . . . Blow on the coal of the heart."[3]

We live in times when often it seems "too dark to see." We stand in utter need of mercy to open the eyes of our hearts to the recurring hope in a fragile forsythia, emerging golden from ashes. With eyes of faith we see, in an apparently flawed creation, life embraced by a God whose name is Mercy, a God always ready to turn our failings and sins into a capacity for deepened compassion. It is mercy that opens the heart of a mother to tenderness for her handicapped child. It opens our eyes to our own handicaps and failures, opens us to embrace the whole wounded world with hearts mercied by the fathomless love of God. Our world desperately needs us to "blow on the coal of the heart" and let God's mercying love enclose, encompass, wind us all round.

Notes

1. All Julian quotations are taken from "The Long Text," *Julian of Norwich: Showings,* trans. Edmund Colledge, OSA, and James Walsh, SJ (Mahwah, NJ: Paulist Press, 1978).
2. Gerard Manley Hopkins, "The Blessed Virgin Mary Compared to the Air We Breathe," in *The Poems of Gerard Manley Hopkins*, 4th ed., ed. W. H. Gardner and N. H. MacKenzie (New York: Oxford University Press, 1970), 94.
3. Archibald MacLeish, *J.B.* (Boston: Houghton Mifflin, 1956), 149–53.

VI

PRAYING MERCY

God's Mercy Is Infinite

Joyce Rupp

"With age-old love I have loved you; so I have kept my mercy toward you."

—Jer 31:3

An age-old love endures no matter what the situation. The Hebrew word for this kind of love is *hesed.* This word translates as either "mercy, compassion, or kindness." What the translations do not include is the fuller meaning, that *hesed* actually implies excessive mercy, compassion, and kindness, far beyond what the human mind can grasp, or believes is possible. *Hesed* is love that overflows with acceptance and kindheartedness.

We humans do not fully realize the vastness of God's mercy. We are too easily swept away with our judgments of both self and others, too quick to condemn and want retribution for those who deliberately hurt us or others. We want to be assured that they've paid the price for their harmful actions and have proven their willingness to change before we approach them with anything other than disdain or contempt.

Not so with God's mercy. Here the message is "Come. You always have a welcome with me. I forgive you. I believe in

From Joyce Rupp, *God's Enduring Presence: Strength for the Spiritual Journey* (New London, CT: Twenty-Third Publications, 2008), 94. Reprinted with permission.

your goodness. I will wait for you to grow and change and, while I do, I accept you with all my heart."

God of excessive mercy, I want to be filled with this same kind of mercy. I want to offer your kind of welcome and forgiveness.

Making Myself Aware of God's Mercy

Joyce Rupp

"For his mercy endures forever."
—Psalm 136:1

The above refrain is proclaimed twenty-six times in Psalm 136 in honor of God's mercy. I used to wonder why the phrase was continually repeated until I realized that the psalmist was emphasizing the endlessness of God's mercy by this constant repetition. The recurring praise of God's mercy is a valuable reminder of the countless times the Holy One has welcomed us back after we have wandered and fallen from the path of goodness. The repetition also serves to convince us that God's mercy will continually be available to us whenever we turn toward this Enduring Love and ask forgiveness for our failings.

I suggest that each of us reflect back on the mistakes, deliberate wrongdoings, poor judgments and decisions we have made that have hurt ourselves or others. After each item that we recall, we can then say: "for your mercy endures forever." By doing so, we will see that our whole life consists of a psalm praising the mercy and kindness of God, extended to us at every moment. This litany of mercy can be

From Joyce Rupp, *God's Enduring Presence: Strength for the Spiritual Journey* (New London, CT: Twenty-Third Publications, 2008), 103. Reprinted with permission.

a powerful experience for anyone who doubts that they are eternally embraced in the Divine Forgiver's arms.

Compassionate One, may the mercy you daily offer me be an incentive to also extend kindness and forgiveness to those who have wronged or failed me.

Kyrie

R. S. Thomas

Because we cannot be clever and honest
and are inventors of things more intricate
than the snowflake—Lord have mercy.

Because we are full of pride
in our humility, and because we believe
in our disbelief—Lord have mercy.

Because we will protect ourselves
from ourselves to the point
of destroying ourselves—Lord have mercy.

And because on the slope to perfection,
when we should be half-way up,
we are half-way down—Lord have mercy.

From R. S. Thomas, *Collected Later Poems,* 1988–2000 (Bloodaxe Books, Ltd., 2004), 135; originally published in 1993. Reprinted with permission from Bloodaxe Books on behalf of the Estate of R. S. Thomas, www.bloodaxebooks.com.

Prayer for Jubilee Year of Mercy

Pope Francis

Lord Jesus Christ,
you have taught us to be merciful like the heavenly Father,
and have told us that whoever sees you sees Him.
Show us your face and we will be saved.

Your loving gaze freed Zacchaeus and Matthew from being enslaved by money;
the adulteress and Magdalene from seeking happiness only in created things;
made Peter weep after his betrayal,
and assured Paradise to the repentant thief.

Let us hear, as if addressed to each one of us, the words that you spoke to the Samaritan woman:
"If you knew the gift of God!"
You are the visible face of the invisible Father,
of the God who manifests his power above all by forgiveness and mercy:

Pope Francis, Prayer composed for the Jubilee Year of Mercy, 5 June 2015.

let the Church be your visible face in the world, its Lord risen and glorified.

You willed that your ministers would also be clothed in weakness
in order that they may feel compassion for those in ignorance and error:
let everyone who approaches them feel sought after, loved, and forgiven by God.

Send your Spirit and consecrate every one of us with its anointing
so that the Jubilee of Mercy may be a year of grace from the Lord,
and your Church, with renewed enthusiasm, may bring good news to the poor,
proclaim liberty to captives and the oppressed,
and restore sight to the blind.

We ask this through the intercession of Mary, Mother of Mercy, you who live and reign with the Father and the Holy Spirit for ever and ever.

Amen.